D1244621

Borrowing Together

In *Borrowing Together*, Becky Yang Hsu examines the social aspects of the most intriguing element of group-lending microfinance: social collateral. She investigates the details of the social relationships among fellow borrowers, and between borrowers and lenders, finding that these relationships are the key that explains the outcomes in rural China. People access money through their social networks, but they also do the opposite: cultivate their social relationships by moving money. Hsu not only looks closely at what transpired in the course of a microfinance intervention, but also reverses the gaze to examine the expectations that brought the program to the site in the first place. Hsu explains why microfinance's "articles of faith" failed to comprehend the influence of longstanding relationships and the component of morality, and how they raise doubts – not only about microfinance, but also about the larger goals of development research.

BECKY YANG HSU (BA Yale, PhD Princeton) is Assistant Professor of Sociology at Georgetown University. Her research interests include religion, organizations, Chinese society, and global development. Her research has received awards from the Eastern Sociological Society and American Sociological Association. She is currently conducting new research on how people define happiness in China, which has been covered by the *Washington Post*.

STUDIES OF THE WEATHERHEAD EAST ASIAN
INSTITUTE, COLUMBIA UNIVERSITY

The Studies of the Weatherhead East Asian Institute of Columbia
University were inaugurated in 1962 to bring to a wider public the results
of significant new research on modern and contemporary East Asia.

Borrowing Together

Microfinance and Cultivating Social Ties

BECKY YANG HSU

Georgetown University

UNIVERSITY PRESS

CAMBRIDGE
UNIVERSITY PRESS

University Printing House, Cambridge CB2 8BS, United Kingdom

One Liberty Plaza, 20th Floor, New York, NY 10006, USA

477 Williamstown Road, Port Melbourne, VIC 3207, Australia

4843/24, 2nd Floor, Ansari Road, Daryaganj, Delhi – 110002, India

79 Anson Road, #06–04/06, Singapore 079906

Cambridge University Press is part of the University of Cambridge.

It furthers the University's mission by disseminating knowledge in the pursuit of
education, learning, and research at the highest international levels of excellence.

www.cambridge.org
Information on this title: www.cambridge.org/9781108420525
DOI: 10.1017/9781108349468

First published 2017

Printed in the United States of America by Sheridan Books, Inc.

A catalogue record for this publication is available from the British Library.

ISBN 978-1-108-42052-5 Hardback

For Edward, Summer, and Zachary

Contents

Figures and Tables

Acknowledgments

In the spring of 2004, I began my stay in the Global Hope (pseudonym) living quarters for staff and visitors. I followed staff when it was practical as they distributed loans in microfinance programs, held meetings with villagers, and kept records. I must first thank the GH staff for allowing me to tag along while they did their work. Living in personnel quarters, staying in the county where I did the fieldwork, and eating nearly all my meals with them, I learned a lot from conversations as we traveled together on foot or by car over unpaved roads; during breakfasts, lunches, and dinners; and while looking through stacks of written records. We became friends and, in some cases, dear ones. I could never have carried out this project if it were not for their willingness to integrate me into their work, which manifested in various ways, including calling me the nickname "Little Hsu" and sharing candidly their thoughts and feelings.

I was a sociology major at Yale University when Deborah Davis took me on my first fieldwork trip to China and Hong Kong. She was the epitome of the fearless researcher. On some days, we tramped up and down dark and dingy stairwells to sit in people's homes and talk about their everyday lives. We hung around brightly lit toy stores and department store displays on other days. I began to love fieldwork then. It was also my first exposure to the close coexistence of the personal and the commercial. Eight years later, I started the fieldwork for this book for my PhD dissertation as a graduate student in the Department of Sociology at Princeton University. I am very grateful to Robert Wuthnow for his generosity, his trust (which made me free to try new things), and his feedback (brilliant and radical insights delivered in a startlingly unpretentious way). Paul DiMaggio, Alejandro Portes, and Viviana Zelizer gave me central questions to consider. I was also fortunate to have Miguel Centeno, Mitchell

Duneier, Michele Lamont, Frank Dobbin, Bruce Western, Gilbert Rozman, King-To Yeung, Mario Small, and Marion Fourcade among my teachers.

This manuscript was written between 2011, when I arrived at Georgetown University as an assistant professor, and March 2017, when I finally completed it. I owe much to my colleagues. Conversations with José Casanova sparked important ideas in this book, and I have been inspired by his ease of movement between sociology, philosophy, and theology. I am grateful to Timothy Wickham-Crowley, Kristen Looney, and Steven Radelet for reading initial drafts of the manuscript. Leslie Hinkson, Brian McCabe, Yuki Kato, William McDonald, Margaret Hall, Dennis McNamara, Kathleen Guidroz, Sarah Stiles, William Daddio, Michael Dyson, Hanadi Salih, and Robert Groves all encouraged me along the way. I am grateful for the enthusiasm and support of Terry Pinkard and Henry Richardson.

During the past three years, I also began fieldwork for a new project on how Chinese people define happiness with my "dream team" of collaborators. I consider it a great privilege to work with them, and this book was written under their influence. I am grateful to Richard Madsen (the exemplar of how to *zuoren*), Deborah Davis (for her empathy and limitless energy), and Anna Sun (truly my friend and colleague) for reading early drafts of the manuscript. I am also thankful for the collegiality of James Farrer and Jay Chih-Jou Chen.

I am grateful for Kimberly Hoang, who read the manuscript closely and gave me excellent comments. I am indebted to others who read chapters, provided feedback, or conversed with me about crucial aspects of the book, in particular Xiaoyang Zhu, Philip J. Ivanhoe, Jessica Teets, Wendy Wolford, Filiz Garip, Amy Reynolds, Steve Offutt, Iddo Tavory, Andrew Perrin, and Christopher Winship.

Research support from the following programs at Princeton University provided the time and financial support for me to write and conduct fieldwork: the Center for the Study of Religion, the Fellowship of Woodrow Wilson Scholars, the Center for Health and

Wellbeing, the Princeton Institute for International and Regional Studies, the Center for Migration and Development, and the Graduate School. The Harvard-Yenching Institute also supported this work.

Parts and precursors to this work were presented at the Development in Question conference of the American Sociological Association's Section on Sociology of Development, Craft of Ethnography workshop, American Sociological Association annual meetings, the Economic Sociology Workshop at Princeton University, the Religion and World Community Seminar at Columbia University, the Social Science Workshop on China at Yale University, and the Center for the Study of Religion workshop at Princeton University. I am grateful to Robert Dreesen, my editor at Cambridge University Press, for his support and to the anonymous reviewers who provided excellent feedback.

The wonderful encouragement from friends and family buoyed my spirits and helped me finish the book. I thank my dad Calvin Yang, my sister Annelise Yang, my grandma Margaret Pan Shuchin Yang (whose vivacity as an artist in her second career inspires me), Wendy Ko, May Long Hsu, Nelson Hsu, Kim Kho, Wendy Hsu, Todd Hayes, Jen Hsu, Dave Hsu, Jean Lee Choi, Stephanie Chang, Michelle Yoon, Hong Park, Christine Kim, Carl Park, Chris Min, Marian Shin, David Cho, Sarra Cho, Ruth Chan, Elizabeth Sohn, Joy Park, and Rosario Ruiz. I remember my mother, Bonnie Yang, who dreamed dreams for me.

Finally, I thank Edward Hsu, who sacrificed more than anyone else to make this book possible. Even more amazing, however, have been his thoughtful daily observations during the past twelve years while I have been writing this book, and his considerate attention to those details. Two little people have joined us since I began this book. Summer is my joy and the only six-year-old in the world who will ever want to read this book. Zachary's soaring exuberance is my delight.

I Social Ties and Microfinance

Predictions for Group Lending

On a cool morning in a midsized village in rural China, I sat with a thirty-six-year-old woman surnamed Lu in the courtyard of her home, which had been built with help from other members of the village, using a rammed-earth technique. She brought out two tiny stools for us to sit on while we spoke. Lu told me matter-of-factly about how the microfinance loan she had gotten (and repaid) was both good and bad. She wasn't sure; she didn't care that much. She had been initially glad to receive the money but found the interest she had to pay a burden. The tiny loan didn't help her with a profit-making enterprise but ended up decreasing her assets overall:

> I repaid by selling my chickens. The loans are good and bad, I guess. It wasn't really very good for us, actually. I didn't do anything with the money, and then I had to pay interest . . . When we had the loans, my sons were small, so I had no extra time to try to do something new. I just used the money for daily purposes or whatever (*suibian yong*).
>
> *(June 8, 10 a.m., field notes)*

Lu's experience confounds the expectation that a microloan leads to increased profit for the borrower. And her response was not unique. Borrowers' reports to me of their experiences with microfinance did not have the characteristics of people empowered. A better description would be indifferent or irritated. Lu didn't know what to call it. Good and bad, she guessed. But not really very good for her, actually.

Ordinary villagers had difficulty repaying the 1,000 RMB ($125) loans, because the mandatory repayment of 60 RMB ($7.50) every two weeks was troublesome. It did not allow for adequate time to make profits from raising livestock (a common venture for the area), since the more profitable animals took months to raise before they could be sold. Social inequality also complicated the program; the influential villagers (those with the most resources and power already) received bigger loans with more flexible repayment schedules. Still they were not making much in profits either. There just are not many options for new enterprises in the villages.

In addition to being practically unhelpful, the program also had what was to Lu an unnecessary and burdensome requirement for borrowers to meet together, according to schedule, as small groups in the village. The meetings had actually been mandated with the goal of increasing the flow of information among borrowers, but in the village, information already traveled as quickly as lightning. The people in her group were her friends and relatives, whom she had lived and worked alongside for many years – they already talked about the loans, and everything else. Even if she had realized that program designers were expecting her to pressure other borrowers to repay their loans (so that the lender would save some of the resources normally spent on monitoring and sanctioning), she would think it a strange presumption. It was not likely she would want to explicitly find fault with a fellow borrower in the village and risk setting off a series of negative reverberations in her own network of social relationships.

According to the microfinance literature, borrowers make profits, people have to be persuaded to repay their loans, and borrowers readily sanction their neighbors when sufficiently incentivized. What I observed ran contrary to these expectations: the borrowers were not making money; rather than needing incentives to repay, most (or all) borrowers repaid, but not because of sanctions; and borrowers simply were not sanctioning each other.

CULTURE AND MICROFINANCE

This book is about what people did with microfinance.

Borrowing Together is a study of what happened in a field site in rural China when there were attempts to have people borrow money, then repay it "together" (using social collateral, pledging their popularity, so to speak, as security for the loan) for the purpose of alleviating their poverty and boosting economic development in their communities. Microcredit, so named for its very small loan amounts, is the best-known type of microfinance and was first launched in China in the 1980s by the United Nations within a larger context of global trends. These loans are granted to very poor people. Although there are many variations, the basic model, made famous by the Grameen Bank, is that the borrower puts the money toward some kind of profitable activity (for example, she buys a sewing machine to set up a tailoring business), keeps most of the profit generated, and uses the rest to repay the loan plus a modest interest. This is thought to both empower borrowers and make them more resourceful, since it demonstrates more respect than a handout. Borrowers get financial rewards (more loans) if all the others in their local group also repay their loans, so people are expected to engage in peer sanctioning to get the loans repaid. It was once a favored solution for those trying to solve the problem of poverty in rural areas but has since led to disappointing results.

When I began the fieldwork in 2004, microfinance was approaching the peak of its popularity, prominent academics were constructing models of why group lending would work, and I was as optimistic as everyone else about microlending's potential. But not long after arriving in the field, I found that what the borrowers were telling me, what the repayment account books indicated, what the staff remarked, and what I observed didn't make sense according to the models – no matter how much I wanted it all to come together neatly. What I saw and what I had read in the books were like ships passing in the night – they seemed to have missed each other completely.

I thought at first that the specificities of the field had "messed up the plan," so I went into problem-solving mode, focusing on the people and issues I thought were gumming up the works. If we were to eliminate the "mess" – the relationships between people, the status differences, the personal histories, the dependencies people had on one another, the friendships, the disagreements between neighbors, the fact that people were significantly more interested in survival than investment – then we could free up the model to work as intended.

Over time, however, I realized that this way of thinking was the very problem with the models. What I was considering peripheral – pesky exceptions to how microfinance should run – were actually *the* decisive factors in the microfinance program. This meant that I had to figure out what people were doing and why. How did they get through life's difficulties? What did they consider admirable and decent? What made them angry, embarrassed, or ashamed, and what did they expect of one another? It was clear that the repayment or default of their loans pivoted on these things. As a sociologist of religion, I was interested in how microfinance intersected with the moral world in which villagers live their lives.[1]

I also began to wonder what, specifically, might be wrong with the microlending models, and *why* there was a conspicuous absence of real people (with feelings and histories and relationships and dependencies) within them. In order to answer this question, I had to investigate the cultural aspects of microfinance itself – that is, what is considered normal, the widely conceded assumptions about reality that form the backdrop of microfinance and upon which its design decisions are based. The more that things were taken as "obvious" or "universally true" – such as the expectation that borrowers are unlikely to repay a loan unless incentivized by the program – the more likely it was that such an assumption would be evidence of culture.

This book is therefore also about culture.

Specifically, it is about how the *person* is conceptualized.[2] More specifically, how are microfinance borrowers (as persons) visualized in group-lending programs – by donors, by development personnel, by themselves? And what are the consequences of these conceptual associations for the repayment of loans, the sanctioning of peers, and the well-being of borrowers? My analytical approach begins with treating the person not as a naturally given entity, but rather as a historically constructed (and possibly problematic) category.[3] Notions of what a person is have, in fact, varied a great deal across times and places.[4] In this book, I focus on the conceptual construction of the person in microfinance, and I look to see how well it predicts the actions of the borrowers in my field site.[5]

So the present exercise not only looks closely at what transpired in the course of a microfinance intervention, it also reverses the gaze to examine the expectations that brought the program to the site in the first place. It investigates the details of the social relationships among fellow borrowers and between borrowers and lenders, finding that these relationships, contrary to existing microfinance theories, are the key that explains the outcomes.

I suggest an explanation of microfinance based on pragmatist theory, which is uniquely able to comprehend the commonsensical Chinese concept of *guanxi*. In doing so, I present an alternative perspective to that which has ruled the day; I focus on how people relate *through* money *to* each other, and not the other way around.[6] *Guanxi* means "relationships" or "social connections," and this mysterious complication, hidden in plain sight, can deflate microfinance plans that depend upon a prescription of whom participants monitor, repay, pressure, and punish. Although *guanxi* is neither a confessed belief nor an allegiance to a faith or god, and it requires no participation or membership in an organized religious institution, it reflects real and important ideas about the way many people make sense of life. It is the context in which people deal with life's biggest moments (like birth and death). *Guanxi* encompasses a point of view that is the basis of moral decisions and everyday judgments about right and wrong, good and bad. A consideration of *guanxi* can shed light on the question of why microfinance models often prove to be limited in its predictions about its borrowers.

That microloans are not turning out as expected is not news. The innovation of group responsibility appealed to donor sentiments, and the apparent no-cost collateral of social pressure appealed to lenders. Optimism was high from the late 1990s to the mid-2000s. It peaked in the late 2000s and then began to plummet approaching 2010. The microcredit climate remains cool today.[7]

Some of the more devastating critiques of past microcredit efforts accuse lenders of actual harm to the already disenfranchised. Some have shown that, in a drive to produce high repayment rates, the Grameen Bank and other microfinance organizations in Bangladesh appropriated honor-and-shame language against women borrowers – making them an object of oppression.[8] Suicides by borrowers in India caused the government in Andhra Pradesh to all but shut down the microfinance industry in 2010 (writing off almost all microfinance loans and issuing strict regulations).[9]

Activity in microfinance, however, has lately been revived, as industry experts have become more careful about profit incentives for lenders and more thoughtful about outsized dreams of mass entrepreneurship. Even so, studies have shown, people are using the cash influxes to smooth out income fluctuations and ensure sufficient daily food and other basic requirements. Microfinance, therefore, is still falling short of its goal to make poor people economically self-sufficient. It instead enters the mix of wages, semiformal or formal loans, and savings and borrowings from family and friends – all funding sources being used to pay for necessities and to weather life's storms.[10]

The number of people living in China on two dollars (or less) a day is approximately 400 million, and approximately 130 million of them live on no more than one dollar a day.[11] Most of them live in rural areas, which do not get the press coverage of the rapidly developing cities. The numbers alone justify close examination of poverty-alleviation efforts in rural China. In addition, this case is also applicable around the globe. People in China live within a power structure where personal ties are both consequential and negotiated, and they practice traditions that feature family and an extended community, including ancestors. This places them in good company with a good portion of the world.[12]

As the title of the book suggests, people cultivate their social ties in microfinance programs. This book is not about how microfinance can change people's lives, but rather, how microfinance is incorporated by people into their networks of social relationships.

CULTIVATING SOCIAL TIES: A PRAGMATIST THEORY
OF MICROFINANCE

In group lending, borrowers are expected to repay if they have financial incentive, and predicted to sanction defaulters in pursuit of these financial incentives. Drawing on John Dewey's essay, "The Moral Self," I build an alternative theory of microfinance that takes social relationships into account.[13] Taking a pragmatic turn would mean that we expect repayment instead to depend on what it does to one's *relationships* (does it improve one's ties?) and what it does to the *self* (is one being a good neighbor?). Three contrasting predictions about how borrowers repay and sanction in microfinance are covered below.

1. Borrowers repay when repayment strengthens important social connections. To understand group lending, the question to ask is how microfinance intersects with a borrower's web of relationships.[14] In rural China, people consciously orient their lives around their relationships (*guanxi*). People's *guanxi*, the social relationships they have cultivated and the networks they are embedded in, define who they are.[15] Social life is therefore not based on agreements and contracts between preexisting entities, but instead, those entities are defined and shaped by the relations between them. We cannot envision "interests" as "the adjustments of isolated selves," Dewey wrote, where "social arrangements were considered to be secondary and artificial."[16]

Social ties (*guanxi*) involve both material obligation and "human feeling" (*renqing*) toward other human beings.[17] Anthropologist Yunxiang Yan writes that *guanxi* constitutes "a total social phenomenon" in the sense that it "provides one with a social space that at once incorporates economic, political, social, and recreational activities."[18] Someone who is good at *guanxi* is someone to be admired. It is a mix of admiration that the person has created and maintained such relationships by treating her friends and family right, but also that she is able to organize it all to the benefit of herself and others, too.[19]

A borrower therefore asks, which of my social ties (*guanxi*) will be affected by my repayment or default?[20] To predict microfinance outcomes, we need to examine the relationships that the borrowing and lending involve. Are there status differences? If the microfinance repayment or default decision touches upon relationships where there are status differences, people will do what they need to do in order to strengthen those connections. Repayment and default will depend on what kind of relationship (*guanxi*) is involved, as well as what kind of relationship the borrower would like to have.

2. Borrowers repay when repaying makes one a good person. Dewey argues that "action manifests and forms the self."[21] Instead of assuming that borrowers are always looking for ways to default, a pragmatist theory of microfinance predicts that the likelihood of default depends on whom the money is going to and what kind of person the action of repaying makes them. Relationships (*guanxi*) are central to the *kind of person* one is. A good son, a good person, takes care of his parents.[22] A good life includes good relationships (good *guanxi*) with parents and children as well as friends and neighbors.

People aim to be the kind of person they want to *become* as they go about their activities and cultivate their relationships. Since every human choice pertains to a future self, "in choosing this object rather than that," Dewey wrote, "one is in reality choosing what kind of person or self one is going to be."[23] There is no such thing as a "fixed, ready-made, finished self"; instead, one's actions determine the person one becomes.[24] Doing good deeds doesn't *reflect* goodness that is within; by doing good, you create yourself as good person.

Whether the borrower feels that people see him as a decent person is part of how he sees himself, and it can happen instantaneously, like seeing a reflection in a mirror. If defaulting has little bearing on whether the borrower feels like a good person, he or she is more likely to default. However, if defaulting means violating a bond of reciprocity and mutual aid between two people, ignoring the emotional attachment that has been generated (perhaps over the span of many years), and not understanding the importance of obligation and indebtedness, then borrowers are unlikely to default.[25]

3. Borrowers avoid sanctioning peers when embarrassing someone incurs a moral cost. *Being* a person is thought of as *becoming* oneself in pragmatist theory. People wonder as they deliberate whether to embarrass or punish someone, *what kind of person would I become if I did that?* People don't like to feel embarrassed, so a tactful and decent person will avoid placing others in this position. A good person refrains from embarrassing people and helps others save face.[26]

People see their lives as interwoven with others, as their shared experiences and their shared past define who they are. In this way, their identity is situated in the latticework of social relationships that constitutes their person. Every act reinforces or diminishes one's social relationships. Since helping people save face is an important part of cultivating good relationships (*guanxi*), it is unlikely that borrowers in rural China sanction each other easily. People's webs of relationships are powerful and longstanding, but also susceptible to injury. In the "giving" and "acquiring" of face and favor, the ongoing reciprocal exchange is central to the moral ordering of relationships, and therefore one's self as a person.[27] If the loan is considered a relatively trivial matter, those who pressure one another about it would be seen as unreasonable or unkind. Someone who seriously considers the reasonableness of sanctioning in the context of *guanxi* would not be quick to predict success for a social-collateral model based on sanctions.

MICROFINANCE AND SOCIAL RELATIONSHIPS

One of the reasons microfinance captivated the attention of donors was its use of "free" collateral: They were excited about having borrowers use social relationships in the service of gaining money and assets. Three axioms of group-lending microfinance are that financial incentives predict repayment; that repayment is not likely, so incentives must be provided via the imposition of interdependency; and that sanctions are costless to apply. These accepted truths have never been questioned.[28]

Borrowing Together reveals that the outcome of microfinance can depend not only on the financial terms of the loans but also how people incorporate microfinance into their existing social relationships (*guanxi*). Repayment and default then become offshoots of the existing ties; this contradicts the expectations that participants would use their social relationships to acquire more loans. Relying on five types of data gathered over three years – "go-alongs" to distribute and collect cash in the villages, interviews, ethnographic observation, microfinance repayment records, and internal reports of the third-sector organization – this book details intriguing outcomes in repayment and peer pressure.

The Grameen Bank's famed group lending model of microfinance describes a means for achieving poverty alleviation and economic development. Does this recipe, cultivated by the organization, its supporters, and academic writing, correspond with the realities for borrowers in the field site in rural China?[29] The recipe is as follows:

Small Loan + Poor Individuals + Group Repayment Incentive =
Self-Regenerating Entrepreneurship

There were two microcredit programs in the field site I observed in rural China, both of which provided small loans to poor individuals with some type of group repayment incentive.

The Grameen replicator was fashioned after the Grameen model (with villagers grouped together in small groups, interest paid early and often, and no more loans disbursed when the larger group fails to repay in full). It was carried out by the Chinese government. Ordinary (noninfluential) villagers indicated that the repayment schedule of the Grameen replicator was not suitable and that the funds they received were not particularly useful for poverty alleviation, *yet* they repaid on time, scraping together the cash even when unable to make a profit (which was most of the time).

The other microfinance program was developed by a third-sector organization that I'll refer to as Global Hope (GH).[30] It had an altered model (as I'll explain) with the intention of fitting better into the realities of village interactions. Rather than needing to be motivated to repay, borrowers in GH's programs considered default "impossible," expressing incredulity at the suggestion of deliberately stiffing a fellow villager serving as guarantor, *even without* programmatic financial incentives.[31]

Repayment

Repayment in the Grameen-replicator program depended on the place of borrowers in the status hierarchy of rural Chinese society. Borrowers repaid their microfinance loans if they needed to improve their relationships with powerful people. The organization of the countryside – where ordinary villagers needed the help of influential villagers and township officials needed their cooperation – led to a "repayment triangle." In this triangle, the influential villagers were at the top (taking out large loans, repaying at their own discretion), the township officials were below them (adjusting repayment schedules to garner goodwill), and the ordinary borrowers were alongside the officials (repaying on time or else signing over their share of the loan to the influential villagers). Status was not only a complicating factor, but also predicted events, but the township government wasn't always in power. Township cadres depend on influential villagers (including current and past village cadres) to "get things done." This dynamic affects the ways that township cadres provide the loans, with larger amounts and indefinite lending periods granted to already more powerful villagers.

In contrast, borrowers repaid in GH's guarantor program because they wanted to be good neighbors. For a long time, national policy (*hukou*) restricted moving elsewhere; people who tried to move out of their officially registered area would be denied essential government services. In addition, the tradition of children remaining near parents and the extended family and the extensive mutual assistance between members of the family meant that the moral universe of the self is created amid longstanding relationships of kinship, friendship, and hostility in the village – "on the village stage." The lack of institutional infrastructure and resources caused, in part, by central-government policies in the past three decades provides yet another reason that villagers depend on one another for survival.

For these reasons, the group incentive structure devised by Global Hope – the guarantor program – had quite astutely transformed the person-to-program debt into a person-to-person one. An influential villager was elected as a guarantor, and this person took on the burden of repayment for the other villagers if they defaulted. Repayment then became a part of being a good person, being a good neighbor; it fit well into the way that villagers treated one another. There was no place for default here, because it would make no sense to treat one's neighbor that way. Borrowers told me that it would be an unthinkable affront not only for the defaulter, but also for those around him or her by association.

Peer Pressure and Sanctions

In both programs, the Grameen replicator and the guarantor program, borrowers avoided direct peer pressure about repayment because causing a fellow villager embarrassment is socially and morally costly. Informal sanctions were frequently used, but they were embarked upon deliberately and only for important personal matters. Borrowers in rural Chinese villages rely on extensive and complex connections with one another as a way of life and as a means of survival. Good management of their web of relationships is the primary tool they have for coping with daily struggles and limited resources, as well as sudden or unforeseen hardship. People are loath to damage the structures that make up their social landscape because they have been carefully shaped and wrought by interactions over long periods of time. People therefore attend carefully to their social interactions, trying very hard to avoid conflict. But it's not just about confrontation; it's about a villager's sense of self. Having good relationships (treating other people right) is how one *is* a good person.

To sanction one's fellow villager leads to a loss of "face" (societal respect) not only for the person sanctioned, but also potentially for oneself. As for formal sanctions, they were rare. The villagers generally settled all of their disputes quite locally, with the input of their family and friends and sometimes the help of a village leader or an elder with moral authority. As a last resort, they had the official grievance process – but it was unreliable and risked alienating important people.

Since loss of face (whether causing or suffering it) diminishes the good social relationships (the good *guanxi* – more on this below) necessary for survival in the village, people try very hard to avoid it. This makes the intended social-collateral mechanism of sanction in the Grameen replicator rather ineffectual. Making and maintaining one's identity requires avoiding embarrassment, so a person wants to avoid losing face for himself. And, if he wants to be a good friend or neighbor, he also helps *others* avoid losing face. So people try very hard not to do anything that might potentially embarrass someone else, in part because it might initiate retaliation but perhaps more importantly because it will make a statement (and not a good one) about who the sanctioner is as a person. The guarantor program, however, used the existing context to its advantage. Not paying back a guarantor would cause a loss of face for everyone involved. No sanction necessary.

OVERVIEW

Chapter 2 describes the beginnings of microfinance as a global-development intervention and its arrival and establishment in rural China. I examine some of the philosophies and assumptions underlying microfinance by focusing on three prominent explanations by development economists for why social collateral should work. To better discuss the premises of microfinance design, I introduce a three-part typology of how we might understand how persons are conceptualized. And I provide further detail about the government Grameen-replicator microfinance program, which is an outgrowth of global development culture, as well as the guarantor program created by Global Hope in the midst of an unstable legal environment for third-sector organizations operating in China.

Chapter 3 delves into the account books and the details of repayment and default in the Grameen replicator loans. The interactions between three strata of rural Chinese society – ordinary villagers, the more powerful influential villagers, and township government officials – were illuminating. The ordinary villagers and township officials both employed the microfinance loans – though in different ways – to strengthen their own relationships with the influential villagers. Within this chapter is a more in-depth discussion of the first aspect personhood construction in my suggested typology: the *unit*. Repayment depended on where the borrower (or lender) was in the power structure. But these important factors did not explain the moral components observed.

Chapter 4 describes the reasons why people always repaid in the second microfinance program. In the guarantor program, people repaid to maintain their friendships with the guarantors. In the villages, people depended upon each other for everyday survival. But people also saw themselves through the eyes of the whole village, and whether the borrower feels that people see him as a decent person happens instantaneously. Consistent with the importance of *renqing* (human feeling) to *guanxi* (human connection), being a good neighbor with genuine friendship loomed importantly as an urgent imperative in their microfinance decisions. In this chapter I talk more about the second aspect of personhood, *separation*, as we look closely at reciprocity in these very close-knit communities.

Chapter 5 examines the costs of sanctions in village life. In contrast to the expectations in microfinance that borrowers can enforce sanctions costlessly – forcing or cajoling other borrowers into repayment – three factors made peer pressure via sanctions very unlikely in this field site. First, the long-term nature of all social relationships in the village meant that conflicts could endure for years and even generations. Second, villagers largely resolved conflicts by their own means; the political structure made going to the village government a last recourse. Finally, sanctions were not isolated incidents but part of village life where social relationships were perceived as an important part of maintaining and/or losing "face." I discuss the third aspect of personhood, *permanence*: People are not fixed entities, nor are people completely self-determined. People can give or take away face from others, and cause them to become someone they don't want to be.

In the conclusion (Chapter 6), I describe the broader implications of this fieldwork – what we can learn from this case that is applicable to understanding microfinance around the world. I also discuss the implications of pragmatist theory for the sociology of development.

Borrowing Together traces in detail what the borrowers and lenders did in the microfinance programs. I show that microfinance repayments and sanctions should be understood as emerging from what they want their relationships to be and the people they want to become. We move now to examine the backdrop behind a number of considerations – the history of microfinance in China, the expectations for group lending, and the origins of the two programs I observed in the field site – that form the context in which borrowers made their decisions in the microfinance programs.

2 Microfinance in China

History, Influences, and Program Efforts

Microfinance in China began when the United Nations brought the approach to rural areas. Eventually, China's national social-science institution and various government agencies and third-sector organizations embraced the efforts and adopted in-country programs. Amid much prestige for microfinance efforts associated with important development institutions, the program model I would later study was delivered to China in the 1980s, where it was assembled, powered up by funding and personnel, and released into a context quite different than what had been pictured by its designers.

The history of microfinance in China can be divided into five periods: its prehistory (1970s), when the famous Bangladesh programs were developed; the period of introduction to and experimentation in China (early 1980s to early 1990s), during which models were created to explain group lending's successes; the expansionary period (late 1990s); the formalization period (early 2000s); and the entrustment period (late 2000s).[1]

THE PREHISTORY: BEFORE 1978

Before the introduction of microfinance, informal finance (including peer-to-peer ROSCAs – rotating savings and credit associations) had been common in China for centuries. Charity was also not a new concept. Historically, individual philanthropists would engage in charitable activities such as mending roads, building bridges, and establishing schools. Well-to-do families maintained crop fields for charitable causes. Alongside these efforts, the government also established facilities for sheltering homeless people, the elderly, the disabled, and orphans. During the Ming and Qing dynasties, these and other charitable associations became more institutionalized.[2]

When the Chinese Communist Party (CCP) assumed power in 1949, the state took complete control over all social, political, and economic activities. There was no clear distinction between the state and the market, and a third sector did not exist. In a social system where children generally provided for elderly parents, the state promised to provide childless seniors food, clothing, housing, medical care, and burial expenses. Shortly after its founding, the new communist government "cleaned up" the public arena, reducing the number of professional associations, religious groups, and merchant organizations so that only a small number of government-sponsored ones remained. Even these were drastically curtailed throughout the socialist era.

Meanwhile, the Grameen Bank, the most highly visible microfinance organization in the world, began to give small loans to poor people in Bangladesh in the 1970s. For these and many other endeavors, it would later receive the Nobel Peace Prize jointly with its founder, Muhammad Yunus, in 2006. As one of the hallmarks of its lending model is the use of social collateral, borrowers form groups and then repay together in a joint-liability structure, where group members are responsible for one another's loans in some form or another. All members may need to repay in order for the group to receive subsequent loans, or the members may take loans in order, on the condition that the previous borrower must repay before the next can borrow. Borrowers are also usually required to meet together and with Grameen staff regularly (once every week or two weeks) to talk about the loans. Microfinance immediately made sense to the experts, donors, and administrators in development institutions, and its endorsement has been helped along by economists' formalized models explaining social collateral.

A TYPOLOGY OF PERSONHOOD FOR MICROFINANCE

In order to better discuss the microfinance models emerging out of the 1970s (and promulgated in the 1980s and 1990s), here I begin delving deeper into the topic of personhood. Why is it so relevant? Because researchers in the social sciences have choices about how to depict the objects of their analysis. Their formalized models reflect specific personhood ideas, producing the core dilemmas of their approaches and shaping their predictions and interpretations. I would contend that concepts of personhood – assumptions about what a person *is* – are always a driving force in the shape of social-science theories, both academic and practical. Beliefs about personhood are embedded in philosophy, psychology, neuroscience, anthropology, sociology, religious studies, and history. A concept of personhood is the part of culture from which suppositions and anticipations are derived, so it sets the terms, so to speak, for theories about social interaction. (These concepts are consequential as they are, but they also have long histories and can change over time.)

I build on the work of others, such as Paul Rabinow, an anthropologist who has analyzed "economics as culture," to examine how microfinance models are an "exotic constitution of reality" that is "historically peculiar," rather than a claim to truth.[3] Let us attempt the tricky task of revealing what has been previously overlooked in microfinance theories by parsing out evidence of personhood philosophies undergirding them. In doing so, I hope to put into proper perspective the specific theory of personhood used in microfinance, whose ubiquitous presence is also visible throughout the social sciences. I'll begin with a typology of sorts – centered on three aspects – to help us talk about an abstract concept in more concrete terms.

The first aspect of personhood, *unit*, is about perception. We can see that in microfinance models, a borrower seen fundamentally as an individual would be expected to weigh costs to and benefits for herself and to arrive at a decision independently of other people and context. In contrast, if one understands a borrower primarily as part of a social network, the analysis would need to extend beyond the individual in order to make sense of her actions.

The second aspect, *separation*, refers to how discrete the person is from other people and things, ranging from isolated to merged. A borrower seen as making decisions based on internal calculations would be expected to think independently from rather than interactively with other people. One baseline assumption would be that it costs him to *find out* whether other borrowers will default; his high separation means low information about others. Another would be that this separation must be addressed by introducing connection – place him in a group that meets and talks often. In contrast, a person who is seen as living and thinking primarily in relation to others, and whose decisions emerge out of interactions, would be expected to be privy to the particulars about a wide range of his fellow borrowers' activities and opinions. He would be seen as already part of a group (or many). Being placed in any new group would then be subject to existing hierarchies, network configurations, or personal relationships.

Permanence describes the extent to which a person is fixed or in flux. A borrower who is modeled as essentially fixed might be expected to be able to do what she wants with no effect on the person she is. So sanctions could be inflicted on fellow borrowers at no profound cost, and using information to force people to repay will make sense if it is in financial interest. However, seeing a borrower as someone who is always potentially changing might lead to the anticipation that she will view repaying a loan as an opportunity to maintain her goodness, while defaulting could decrease it (as might antisocial behavior such as sanctioning).

In the Grameen design for group-lending microfinance, we find an assumption that borrowers will not normally repay a loan – thus the social-collateral design is considered sensible. This reveals a concept of *unit* as quite individualistic and a concept of *permanence* as quite fixed. There is also the assumption that the borrowers do not see each other often or know each other well – hence the action of putting them into groups and mandating frequent meetings. This stems from a view of the person as very *separated*. Cultural evidence shows that people already quite efficiently organize themselves, without the help of a bank or a third-sector organization. Yet the typical group-lending design presumes that their just-created groups can trump the administrative hierarchies the borrowers are already in or the obligations formed in preexisting, cross-cutting, generations-old networks.

Experimentation in a Changing Environment:
1978 to the Early 1990s

In 1978, Deng Xiaoping's economic reforms marked China's break with earlier fiscal policy. Beginning in the 1980s, the central government decentralized fiscal policy, granting more control to local governments. The rural population ceased working in communes and work units, and the government withdrew from many social services it used to provide. Public goods like education, health care, and infrastructure became local responsibilities. However, these mandates were largely unfunded, and local governments were not allowed to issue debt or run fiscal deficits. Moreover, the central government restricted the ability to tax local populations. Rural officials were expected to find ways to provide public services to the population with few revenue sources, and their promotion depended on public-goods provision. Many took to taxing illegally. Many went into debt.

These social and economic changes had left China in need of new solutions. Faced with a gaping hole between the demand and supply of public services – and dependent on taxes from a largely impoverished population – township officials began to tap the resources of eager-to-help third-sector organizations. There was a desire to reap the benefits of much-needed assistance but also a cautious vigilance against any signs of mobilization for political change. These new partnerships were tenuous, but local- and central-government officials were willing to feel their way toward potential solutions to their growing development needs.[4] Third-sector organizations have thus received contradictory signals from the party-state. While in practice, the government has shown tolerance toward them (especially at the local government level), it has enacted restrictive legislation to ensure that they do not undermine the leadership of the Chinese Communist Party.[5] Since the laws are inconsistently applied, some organizations have been able to operate in-country while others have been denied access.

The United Nations was one early organization that had success gaining entrée. In 1981, microfinance in China as we know it today – with its connections to international development, specific funding sources, and programmatic forms – began when the UN's International Fund for Agricultural Development (IFAD) sought to apply their microfinance experience to rural China. One year later, the UN Development Fund for Women (UNIFEM) added microfinance as part of its efforts in China to help improve the quality of women's lives. Within the next decade, other parts of the United Nations system followed suit, including the UN Fund for Population Activities (UNFPA), UN Children's Fund (UNICEF), UN Development Programme (UNDP), and World Food Programme (WFP).[6]

In 1986, the Chinese government established the Leading Group Office of Poverty Alleviation and Development (LGOP) of the State Council, an interministry body reporting to the highest level of government.[7] The LGOP began subsidizing poverty-loan programs administered to poor counties. These years were also characterized by experimentation, as the Chinese Academy of Social Sciences (CASS), the premier national social-sciences organization in China, teamed up with LGOP to test the feasibility of group-liability lending programs modeled after those of the Grameen Bank.[8]

Modeling Group Lending

Meanwhile, in global development, microfinance had become well established, and economists began to try to model reasons why it was believed to be highly successful. In 1990, the American economist Joseph Stiglitz, an enormously influential voice in global development research and practice, published an article in *The World Bank Economic Review* about the role of peer monitoring in microcredit programs. "Peer Monitoring and Credit Markets" has been cited almost 1,800 times (he has been cited over 240,000 times total), and its model is used by those who write microfinance handbooks and those who teach classes about microfinance at places such as the Harvard Kennedy School.[9] Stiglitz was later awarded the Nobel Memorial Prize in Economic Sciences in 2001 for his work on information asymmetries and has been the chief economist of the World Bank and chair of the US President's Council of Economic Advisers.

Stiglitz's famous article offered a general theory of peer monitoring, an analysis for why the Grameen Bank's group-lending program should work. Repayment is not automatically likely, he argued, so in order to enhance repayment, institutional lenders (banks) have the problem of making sure that borrowers use the funds prudently. A solution that may partially solve this problem is having neighboring borrowers answer for each other; if your neighbor goes bankrupt, you pay a penalty to the bank. The Grameen Bank of Bangladesh and similar group-lending programs elsewhere successfully use peer monitoring, Stiglitz reminds his reader, leading to their thriving financial performance. Later in the article, Stiglitz swaps the bank for government, suggesting that either could be the source of an effective lending program.

The site of action, in Stiglitz's model, is the mind of the individual. The causal force resides in the borrower's internally made decision. It is not important at all who the lender is; the role can be played as well by government as by the nameless, faceless "bank," which is the closest thing to context in the model. Stiglitz focused on asymmetries of information because he, like many social scientists, regards formalized information flow as critical for the collection of data. Understanding the microfinance decision as one primarily of individual calculation lends validity to the expectation that the borrower has no preexisting obligations or connection. The program is therefore eminently powerful, able to create the only incentive that will be used in the borrower's internal calculus by imposing the constraint of social collateral (through the yoking together of fellow borrowers).

Five years after the publication of Stiglitz's paper, Timothy Besley and Stephen Coate published a paper in the *Journal of Development Economics* with a similar goal of trying to explain Grameen group lending. The two economists were (at the time) at the Woodrow Wilson School at Princeton and the Wharton School at the University of Pennsylvania. Cited almost 1,500 times, their paper examined the impact on repayment of lending groups, in which members are made jointly liable for repayment. With the aim of understanding how joint liability affects borrowers' decisions, they set up lending-group repayment as a game based on situational incentives:

> The concern here is with whether grouping borrowers together, and making them jointly liable in this way, improves repayment rates. Clearly, it introduces interdependence between the two borrowers' decisions. Borrower 1, for example, may decide to repay the entire loan himself if he believes that borrower 2 will pay nothing. But if borrower 2 believes this is the case then he has no incentive to pay his share. To answer the question, we must model the *repayment game* to which group lending gives rise.[10]

In this model, Besley and Coate presumed that borrowers are independent unless the microfinance program "introduces," as the two academics put it, interdependence among them. In the repayment game they modeled, social relationships between individuals were not addressed or even considered. Prior interdependencies were not a factor. The person is conceptualized as separate from the quality of his longstanding relationships with other people and his environment. Borrowing and lending is framed as a contract between independent elements, rather an outgrowth of the relationship between the borrower and lender. Repayment, in Besley and Coate's view, does not carry any meaning to the relationship with that person, and therefore has nothing to do with the kind of person one is.

Expansion: The Late 1990s

While academics modeled microfinance through the 1990s, an expansionary period began in China. LGOP's participation in microfinance prefigured a positive response from several large sections of the central government. In September 1996, the Central Committee of the Chinese Communist Party and the State Council convened a high-level meeting in order to discuss the national poverty-alleviation strategy. By the end of the year, microfinance pilot projects in China funded by national and international sources had reached about 90 million RMB ($11.25 million).

In February 1998, the head of the national strategy stated his support during a national-level meeting: "Microfinance is an effective tool to reduce poverty. We should experiment with microfinance projects in some areas and then spread these projects to other areas. The key characteristic of microfinance operations is that funds directly reach the poorest rural households and that the rate of repayment is high."[11] As a result, funding was allocated to commence or expand microfinance projects. In October, the CCP's Central Committee on Agriculture and Rural Areas decided to expand microfinance projects. By the end of 1998, government funding alone for poverty-reduction loans was 600 million RMB ($75 million). According to the Office of the Leading Group for Economic Development in Poor Areas, by August 1998, 605 counties in twenty-two provinces were involved in government microfinance programs.[12]

Through the 1990s and 2000s, the official legal status of third-sector organizations in China remained unstable, as evidenced by the government's history of carrying out large-scale "clean-up and rectification" campaigns against them in 1950, 1990, and 1997.[13] At the same time, however, the government was increasingly signaling its support of charitable organizations. In 1994, the *People's Daily* newspaper, part of the official Chinese media apparatus, declared, "Socialism needs its own charitable undertakings and its own philanthropists."[14] An inclusion of public-interest donations in income-tax deduction in 1994 was followed by tax deductions for enterprises and institutions in 1997. Township officials, meanwhile, were engaging in a variety of partnerships and collaborations with third-sector organizations like Global Hope.

Toward the late 1990s, the LGOP worked to more closely duplicate models of international microfinance, but after the changes, the repayment rates only increased a little, to just under 62 percent (in 1997).[15]

Formalization: The Early 2000s

That same year, a UNDP report noted that the institutional features of rural China would make replication of Grameen-style microfinance difficult.[16] Government bodies responded by issuing more regulations and guidelines, and so the formalization period began. The central government began laying the foundation for more of the nation's formal financial institutions to take part in microfinance activity, and the regulatory environment for microfinance was solidified.

The legal standing of third-sector organizations working in China, however, was still ambiguous. In 2003, representatives from the Ford Foundation, Citi Foundation, and attendees from over one hundred microfinance programs in China met together at the first China Microfinance Summit. Afterwards, they decided to create the China Association of Microfinance (CAM) together. Regulations stated that associations needed to be subordinate to a government department. The Ministry of Commerce agreed to be the government department responsible for CAM.[17] Citi Foundation continued to provide support, committing to five years of helping to establish CAM in partnership with CASS, even though microfinance projects from the first two periods were beginning to fall apart.

In the meantime, Chinese state-owned commercial banks had been gradually closing their branches at the county level and lower. Between 1995 and 2004, nearly half of the branches of the four largest of these banks closed down (about 77,000 remained).[18] At the same time, state-owned banks were restricting the ability of the remaining rural branches to disburse loans. Since 2000, these branches have only been able to collect savings.

The Microfinance Establishment: The Late 2000s

The late 2000s brought a change to policy and the legal environment. The central government encouraged third-sector organizations to work with commercial microfinance institutions, and it also endorsed rural financial efforts (the creation of village banks, lending companies, and rural mutual-credit cooperatives). In 2010, it was estimated that the combined portfolio of all microfinance institutions run by third-sector organizations in China was worth approximately 1 billion RMB ($125 million) and served approximately 150,000 active clients.[19]

As of 2014, there were 8,000 registered microcredit institutions in China, and CAM was advocating for better institutionalization of microcredit (since third-sector organizations remained vulnerable with no explicit laws), noting that there were some examples of leading microfinance programs run very well by third-sector organizations.[20] Today, third-sector organizations are still not protected by law, but aspects of recent history enable them to remain and operate: national policies on microfinance and poverty alleviation, international cooperative agreements, and official approval of experiments of poverty alleviation and financial innovation.

Theorizing about Sanctions

By the time microfinance efforts in China were well established, economic models of microfinance had also crystallized. Beatriz Armendáriz and Jonathan Morduch published *The Economics of Microfinance* in 2010 for students, researchers, and practitioners, summarizing the state of the art twenty years after Stiglitz's article. The preface of the book notes that the authors drew from their own experiences: Armendáriz had founded the first replication of the Grameen Bank – the Grameen Trust Chiapas – in Mexico in 1996. Morduch had advised projects at Bank Rakyat Indonesia, carried out research in Bangladesh, and helped collect and analyze data in Chinese villages on politics, growth, and inequality. Their book featured a chapter on group lending, which includes a section that predicts repayment as a factor of the costs to the borrower of monitoring a peer and the cost of the sanction to the peer who is being monitored. They did not pay much attention to what goes into the cost of the sanction *to the borrower who is doing the monitoring*. Writing of y as gross return (the rate of return on an investment), they surmised,

Group lending with peer monitoring can, however, induce each group member to incur a monitoring cost k ex post to check the actual revenue realization of her peer. *We assume that with this information, the partner can force the peer to repay.* Let us assume that by incurring a cost k, a borrower can observe the actual revenue of her peer with probability q, and let d denote a social sanction that can be applied to a borrower who tries to divert due repayments. Then, if R denotes the gross interest rate set by the bank, a borrower will choose to repay if and only if $y - R > y - q(d + R)$, or equivalently, $R < [q/(1-q)]d$. . . . Specifically, a borrower will choose to monitor her peer whenever the monitoring cost k is less than her expected gain qy from avoiding the need to assume responsibility for her peer's repayment. Thus, joint responsibility makes lending sustainable by inducing peer monitoring and overcoming enforcement problems associated with ex post moral hazard.[21]

The repayment model, where sanctions are costless and are acceptable in any moral context, revealed a theory of personhood that regarded the individual as highly fixed (the third aspect of the typology, permanence). This borrower is theorized to remain the same regardless of what he does. The model divulged no sense that people are aware that their actions are part of the person they become. Armendáriz and Morduch assumed that there is no cost to sanctioning one's neighbors and peers, so that with certain kinds of information, the partner of the borrower can "force the peer to repay."

THE TWO MICROFINANCE PROGRAMS OF THIS STUDY

My fieldwork takes place in the 2000s, at the height of microfinance's perceived success, supported by the sophisticated models that had emerged from prestigious institutions. At that time, the Chinese government was trying out its own microfinance programs while allowing third-sector organizations to do so as well. The villagers who took part in the microfinance programs had previously relied mostly on informal loans from friends and family, though some had had access to more formal loans offered by rural credit cooperatives.[22] Programs like Global Hope's survived by working cooperatively with the rural government to try to achieve the poverty alleviation that both groups desire. And the government-run program I observed in the same county was part of a large, decade-long rollout of Grameen replicators carried out with the government as lender. To fully understand the results of the government's rather long-lasting experiment, we need to understand two dominant social contexts in rural China: the political-administrative structure and the priority of personal relationship networks.

Party-State Structure in Rural China

The Chinese government implemented the commune system of collectivized agriculture in the 1950s, including the pooling of income. In the communes, labor was organized into work crews, and people were assigned jobs and awarded points for their efforts. In return for the labor, the state supplied food, occasionally redistributed cash, and provided basic welfare. Life in some villages was characterized by constant bickering over the allocation of work points and assignment of jobs, as individuals felt driven to protect their rights, lest the system favor others.[23]

In rural China, cadres supervised all work and distributed all resources for basic needs. In this way, cadres controlled a monopoly. During radical periods, villagers needed to seek permission from cadres even for social activities such as visiting relatives and going to marketplaces. Complaints about cadres were punished with accusations of counterrevolutionary activities, and higher levels of government rewarded cadres with social and political status as well as extra resources. At the same time, as sociologist Richard Madsen has described, the honest cadre – dedicated to the collective welfare of the village – was an accepted ideal and a source of legitimacy, allowing cadres to exercise power.[24] During its hegemony in China, communist ideology was an effective way to justify cadre actions and breadth of authority.[25] The villagers lived in what sociologist Andrew Walder has called a state of "organized dependency" on cadres.

After reforms in the 1980s, rural life returned to the peasant-farming system, reducing the farming scale and renewing farmers' focus on self-sufficiency.[26] Decollectivization restructured village life to make the villager-cadre relationship more contingent on their interpersonal interactions.[27] Although agriculture shifted from the collective back to the household unit, the earlier collective unit remained as an organizational structure for state welfare allocation (thus the "administrative village," which comprises several natural villages). At the end of 2006, there were a total of 37,000 townships (formerly called "communes"), 624,000 administrative villages, and 740 million village dwellers in 249 million households.

Levels of local government are organized first by province, then prefecture, then county, township, and administrative village (see Table 2.1). Townships have a population of around 10,000 and are governed by a mayor, an assistant mayor, a party secretary, often an assistant party secretary, and a handful of staff. (Together, these are the "township officials" discussed in this book.) Township Microfinance Offices administered the loans, set the terms, and approved extensions to repayment schedules.

Administrative villages (formerly "brigade") range in population from 1,000 to 5,000 and are governed by a village committee made up of three to seven cadres. These influential villagers, in addition to being members of the village (farmers themselves), are paid for their service on the committee and may also be members of the Chinese Communist Party. According to the *Organic Law of the Villagers Committees of the People's Republic of China*, village committee members are elected directly by villagers to terms of three years (and may continue to hold office indefinitely if reelected). Overseen by the township government, they are to manage public affairs and public welfare, mediate disputes, and maintain public order.[28]

The township government draws on local taxes paid by villagers to create a basic salary and bonuses for the village cadres. These bonuses compose the bulk of their cadre income and are dependent upon the completion of tasks, such as supervising spring plowing.

Table 2.1 *Administrative and political structure of field site*

| Administrative Division | Government | Cadres of the Party-State | Third-Sector |
		Chinese Communist Party	Organization*
Central Government			
Province			
Prefecture			
County			
Township	• mayor	• (township) party secretary	• director
Administrative Village	• assistant mayor	• assistant party secretary	• program manager
(Natural Village)**	• staff	• party staff	• staff
	• village head	• (village) party secretary	• village liaisons
	• village committee members	• village committee members who are party members	
	• informal authority figures: heads of clans, moral leaders		

* This has authority over administration of specific poverty-alleviation programs only.

** Natural villages are not official administrative divisions, but naturally occurring clusters of homes.

Cadres may also be punished with fines of the same amount if they fail. Consequently, those who take up the role of village cadre tend to do so only if they think they can get the other villagers to do what they say.

The village cadres collect taxes, play the role of police, document households, and implement government policies (including forced family-planning policies). Additionally, they control the allocation of land and of relief funds, the pooling of villager money, the use of profits from collective enterprises, the granting of labor contracts and licenses, and the distribution of water and electricity. Their power is especially important where neither property rights nor legal systems are clearly defined. Since policy changes have decreased the direct supervision of these leaders by the next-higher administrative level (township officials), getting on a village leader's good side is even more important for the less powerful.

Abuses can be carried out by village cadres without much consequence, but they can also grant favors to those who need a bit of help. Since cadres can only succeed in their tasks if they are well liked or at least respected by the other members of the village, they realize that they must be judicious about their moves. The cadres are generally supervised very loosely, but sudden sanctions from above can arrive with no warning. Then again, campaigns mandated from higher up could sometimes be completely ignored, with no consequences.[29]

Guanxi, *Personal Networks, and Institutional Change*

Social relationships in the villages of rural China have remained so important partly because of the longstanding tradition that adult children settle near to their parents, so villages are often organized by kinship. In these (sometimes very large) family units, individuals both provide aid to and benefit from family members. The national policy of household registration (*hukou*), set up in 1958 by the Chinese Communist Party to regulate the economy and control internal migration,[30] means that families are registered in a geographic location and are denied essential government services if they move away (exceptions are made for marriage). Although people now migrate unofficially and can even get a job without the valid permits, it is technically illegal for those in rural areas to change their residence (all land is the property of the state and cannot be bought or sold). The same families have been living in the same village for nearly sixty years.

Changes in power relations since reform have also caused an increase in the importance of *guanxi* networks; because the state has retreated, *guanxi* is more important now than in the socialist era. People maintain personal networks that include kin and friends both within and outside of the village. Gift-giving, particularly during institutionalized rituals of weddings and funerals, facilitates cooperation and self-protection for villagers. (Households spend nearly 20 percent of their annual income on gifts.)[31] After decollectivization (when land was no longer farmed by collectives but was given back to families for oversight), farmers became independent producers and therefore needed to coordinate with others for mutual assistance to do many things, including purchasing seeds, clearing financial hurdles, harvesting, and selling at market. In situations where a villager comes into conflict with agents of the local government, those with a better network have a measure of protection not enjoyed by the less popular.

THE GRAMEEN REPLICATOR

Into this context was begun the Grameen-replicator microlending program I observed. It was a government program with directives at the national level and implementation by township cadres at many different sites. True to the Grameen model, loans in the program were very small, lasted for only one year, and had a low interest rate. Target clients were the poorest of citizens – farmers living in the villages. See Table 2.2[32] for a summary of the microfinance industry in China by type of institution, including government, third-sector, and commercial.

Like a majority of the government programs in China, the program I observed did not use traditional collateral but social collateral.

Table 2.2 *Microcredit suppliers in China*

Type of Institution	Target Clients	Traditional Collateral	Average Loan Size (RMB)*
Third-Sector Organizations	mid- to low income and poor	no	300–3,000
Agricultural Bank of China	mid- to low income and poor	no	3,000
Rural Credit Cooperatives	all kinds of farming households	no, but yes for large loans	3,000–30,000
Village/Township Banks	citizens and micro/small enterprises	yes	3,000–300,000
Rural Mutual Credit Cooperatives	member farmers and enterprises	no	3,000
Poverty Alleviation Loans	mid- to low income and poor	no	3,000
China Postal Savings Bank	all kinds of farming households	no, or pledge only	3,000–300,000
People's Bank of China	citizens and small enterprises	yes	3,000–300,000
Commercial Banks	citizens	no	30,000

Source: Du (2008a).

* approximate amounts for purposes of comparison

Its loan size of 1,000 RMB falls at the small end of the range, since most of the microloans in China are several thousand RMB, and they can range into hundreds of thousands.[33] The interest rate was not zero (the lowest offered by the government), but it was quite low at 3 percent, which a majority of the other government programs also provided. But compounded every two weeks, the interest still totaled over 100 RMB by the end of the loan.

Three leaders – head, accountant, and cashier – were elected in each administrative village to help collect the money and keep records. Self-selected groups of five borrowers each (the program's version of the self-help groups highlighted in studies of microfinance elsewhere) were also formed for meetings and collection of funds. The five borrowers represented their nuclear families, and one member of the group was then elected small-group leader. All of the borrowers in all the groups in the administrative village had to completely repay before anyone in the administrative village could take another loan. The small groups met every two weeks, at which time partial payment was collected by the small-group leader.

The money for the loans followed the lines of the political structure. Funds were initially distributed by large government bureaus to the township Microfinance Offices, which then administered the programs within the administrative villages, with the help of the village committees. Repayment funds were delivered by the small-group leader to the cashier of the administrative village, who then deposited the money with the township Microfinance Office. From there, the money was to be returned to the central government.

The staff assigned to microfinance administration varied by township – in some places, there was a specific person designated for microfinance, while in others, I observed the assistant mayor and the assistant party secretary handling the task of gathering late repayments.

GUARANTOR PROGRAM

The GH microfinance program was similar in many ways to others produced by third-sector organizations. No collateral was required in order to receive the loan of 1,000 RMB (an amount toward the smaller end for third-sector organizations; see Table 2.2). The annual interest rate was 8 percent (again, less than the mean). Like the Grameen replicator, the GH program was administered at the administrative-village level, with three elected leaders. However, several character-istics most notably distinguished GH's program: the social-collateral structure did not involve small groups but was rather based on one group *guarantor* in each administrative village, the lending period was eight months instead of one year, and repayment was collected only once (at the end), along with interest (compounded once and equaling 80 RMB).

The guarantor of the GH program was one elected villager, who in addition to assisting with distribution and collection of the funds, also agreed to personally guarantee their repayment. Also elected were two assistants to the guarantor – a cashier and an accountant – who pledged a degree of responsibility themselves (see Table 2.3). Together, they agreed to repay on behalf of any borrower in the administrative village who might default. In other words, defaulting on the loan effectively changed the debt from a person-to-program obligation to a person-to-person one.

The records for the guarantor program indicated 100 percent repayment, but this must be interpreted in light of the clear selection bias: Unless a guarantor and his or her assistants were elected and agreed to the terms, the program did not get under way in that area. Therefore the villages where there were already social networks that tended to work with the guarantor system were the only ones where the program existed. (Also it should be noted that 100 percent repay-ment to Global Hope doesn't necessarily mean 100 percent repayment by defaulters to the guarantor who had covered them. These repay-ments rates were not measured by GH.)

The organization of Global Hope's microfinance program was unique because of the organization's uncertain legal status, so study-ing their efforts provides important detail about the realities of third-sector work in nondemocratic environments.[34]

Table 2.3 *Administrators of two microfinance programs in the field site*

Administrative Division	Grameen Replicator	Guarantor Program
Central Government		
Province		
Prefecture		
County		• GH microfinance
Township	• assistant mayor or	coordinator
Administrative Village	assistant party	• GH program manager
(Natural Village)	secretary	• township-level GH
	• Microfinance	and government staff
	Office staff	• guarantor (elected by
	• other township	village)
	staff	• cashier (elected by
	• head (elected by	village)
	village)	• accountant (elected
	• cashier (elected by	by village)
	village)	
	• accountant	
	(elected by village)	
	• small-group leader	
	(elected by five-	
	person group)	

Little Wen was the director of Global Hope for the county area during my study. She had impressively managed, in the midst of government control, to carve out a situation that allowed her to bring in resources, innovate new programs, and provide real help to people. She worked with the government's village committees to distribute necessities to a broad portion of the population. She worked through local channels to call meetings for GH programs (like microfinance, but also others) and to spread information about GH-sponsored training and education sessions.

Little Wen's role was interwoven into the government structure almost seamlessly. She sometimes supervised township officials for specific projects. Villagers generally conflated the two groups, calling Global Hope "the part of the government that does good things" (July 28, 12 p.m., field notes). In the GH county headquarters, Little Wen oversaw activities in the seven townships where GH worked (out of the county's sixteen townships). There were twenty staff members working in her office, including five fully integrated government workers who also reported to the county government (their paychecks came from the county, but otherwise, they worked for Little Wen). They showed up reliably and respectfully and worked as diligently as did the GH employees. Everyone in the office wanted to provide services that the rural poor needed, and the natural conduit for these services – the only path to reach them – were appendages of the local state.

Little Wen's approach was effective, but GH's relationship to the party was still characterized by wariness. One township party secretary had been heard insinuating to a visitor that GH "didn't like the party" (June 6, field notes). But Little Wen was not worried. About a year prior, she recounted to me, the government had formally examined Global Hope's activities. Acknowledging that villagers welcomed GH but didn't necessarily welcome the party, they had been worried that GH was instigating political activity. What they found was that "GH was just improving everyday life for the villagers" (June 6, field notes). For officials concerned about maintaining legitimacy with the rural population, these improvements could only help them in reaching their goals.

CONCLUSION

Over the past four decades, group-lending microfinance was designed in Bangladesh, became popular worldwide in global development circles, and was brought in its current form to China by the UN and third-sector organizations. Due to its steep rise in popularity, microfinance also became a project of the Chinese government in the 1990s. In the meantime, academics were creating models to explain group lending's successes. Microfinance activities expanded and were formalized in the late 1990s and early 2000s.

The millennia-old history of centralized government in China, mixed with a more recent openness to creative poverty-alleviation solutions, has created a unique context for microfinance. There have been large-scale, government-directed initiatives but also quite a bit of space at the local level for officials to do as they wish, which may include working with third-sector organizations. This paradox was visible in the two microfinance programs I observed: the Grameen replicator was part of a massive rollout of government programs that had mixed application success, and the guarantor program was created by a third-sector organization that had the leeway to adapt and tailor their program to social patterns in the villages. Both operated along governmental lines of authority, at the level of the administrative village. Both were motivated by the international acclaim given to Grameen and to microfinance more generally.

We move now to examine the Grameen replicator in more detail. It had its impetus at the level of the central government, and its borrower-lender relationship was between the township officials and villagers (both village cadres and those with less clout).

3 Credit and Favor

Social Structure, Repayment and Default

Villagers who participated in the Grameen replicator microfinance program might use their 1,000 RMB (about $125) to buy four piglets for 200 RMB ($25) each at the beginning of the year for a total of 800 RMB ($100), use the remaining 200 RMB for pig food and care, and then sell the adult pigs eight months later for 1,100 RMB ($137.50) each, generating a profit of 3,400 RMB ($425) before paying interest on the loan. Since the average income was about forty-nine cents a day, this would be making twenty-eight months' profit in eight months. Piglets can get sick (requiring costly medicine) and sometimes die, so the profit is not guaranteed. But raising pigs is something that most villagers do anyway, so they know what to expect and how to navigate these challenges.

However, this formula begins to break down when other realities are factored in. If a borrower decides to buy piglets using the loan, it will take eight months to raise them. So until then, at each twice-a-month meeting, she must scrape together an extra 46 RMB for partial repayment. The unspent 200 RMB could cover two months of repayment (unless it's needed for pig care or pig medicine). For the remaining four months, the borrower must find an extra 92 RMB per month – a grand total of three-and-a-half weeks' pay.[1] If the borrower can make it to the end of the program, she will sell the adult pigs and make a good amount of money. But if the pigs die (as they sometimes do), the borrower is really in a pickle.

Chickens are less risky; 1,000 RMB buys a lot of chickens, and then the chicks come quickly. But a borrower who decides to play it safer and settle for chickens will make a smaller profit, as each chicken only sells for 4 RMB. That means that for each of the repayments scheduled every two weeks, a borrower needs to sell twelve chickens. But sell to whom? She'll have to go to market. Getting that many chickens out to the market is a tremendous effort ... unless she has a truck (unlikely). If her neighbor is one of the more well-off villagers, *he* may have a truck. He might even let her use it, but favors are always reciprocal. The borrower would now be indebted not only to the program but to her neighbor.

My observations of the Grameen replicator program were based on interviews with borrowers, data from account books, and interactions with administrators and staff – from village cadres to township officials. They showed that repayment depended upon the location of the borrower in the larger structure of status differences and stratification. This put to the test the assumptions of the group-lending models, which make the individual, spurred to entrepreneurship, the main unit of analysis without regard to social context. To understand the Grameen replicator in particular requires an investigation of how borrowers cultivated their *guanxi* in relation to power, prestige, and even survival.

TOO POOR FOR MICROFINANCE

"The Time Was Too Short"

In one group interview, five men and two women told me how they work together to make life easier. But sometimes they have to choose between working together at home and going out to find work individually: "Yes, we do things together," they all said, chiming in, "like planting crops, feeding pigs. But we can't always sell our pigs, so many of us have gone out to look for work. After so many people have left to work, we haven't been doing as much work together."

Since economic reforms, an estimated 340 million people have moved from rural areas to urban areas (or attempted to do so) in search of work – likely the largest migration in human history.[2] However, the success of these efforts have varied; I heard during fieldwork that many in the field site only go out for a few months at a time, returning home when the work dries up. These efforts have provided some extra cash flow, but it's not always enough to cover expenses.

In one of the small groups, one person had trouble paying, so we repaid for them for the time being, and they repaid us later. We've only gotten loans like that once, so that only happened one time ... when we got 1,000 RMB, and had to pay some back every fifteen days ... [One of the two women:] The time ... was too short ... if I had bought a cow with the loan, it wouldn't have grown enough to sell yet, but I still had to repay.

(June 6, 4 p.m., field notes)

Money was not easily made in the villages, and profit was neither quick nor guaranteed. There were few opportunities to create successful new businesses for rural people. Unfortunately, the microcredit ideal is a loan earmarked for entrepreneurship. (As a banner on the United Nations website for 2005, the Year of Microcredit, asked, "How could you start a business if you could not get credit?")[3] But this loan had a schedule that made it quite difficult to carry out even the most common method of making money in the villages: raising livestock. The woman who said that *if* she had bought a cow with the money, her plan wouldn't have worked out seemed to have had the idea, made the calculation, and, disappointed, decided against it – a far cry from entrepreneurial inspiration.

"I Took Out the Loan Because I Got Sick"

The hope for microlending as a natural impetus for the human entrepreneurial spirit initially meant that borrowers, brimming with ideas, would embody economic gumption: anyone can make it with just a little help if she works hard enough. "All human beings are entrepreneurs. When we were in caves, we were all self-employed. We were finding food, we're feeding ourselves," said Muhammad Yunus in an interview shortly after receiving the Nobel Peace Prize.[4] Innovative activities were considered something that poor people all over the world were already engaging in – only in the informal economy rather than the market. Therefore, by channeling their work into the free market, microcredit would help propel them to become bona fide entrepreneurs.

But the people in the villages did not react that way. Most of the borrowers who did try to turn a profit used the money for livestock, which was not a new idea. But *most* of the borrowers actually used the money to cover expenses rather than to invest in a venture. Villagers agreed that while putting the entire loan amount toward a profit-generating activity would have been ideal, in their cash-strapped situations, they had more pressing matters, such as health and the education of their children. A thirty-eight-year-old man told me that he took the loan in order to pay his medical bills and to send his child to school. With a colloquial, tongue-in-cheek irritation, he explained his priorities:

> I took out the loan because I got sick and needed to pay the medical bills. Also, I have to send my child to school – every ten days, he wants 500 RMB! That son is in middle school. I have to pay too much for him. My beard is so bitter that it is getting long (*huzi kude hen chang*).
>
> *(June 8, 9 a.m., field notes)*

"We Used the Money to Eat"

The ideal in microfinance design is that the loan money is "extra," set apart for investing in future benefit. And microfinance certainly endorses this kind of longer-term gratification. But does it assume a basic financial stability that might not be present? The borrowers were in a situation of highly variable cash flow, so they typically mixed their savings and borrowings, using them to provide food and other requirements for survival in daily life.[5] Temporality is experienced differently when present needs outweigh possible future usefulness. When villagers did have extra, they might lend to another who is strapped for funds. When they were strapped, they might borrow to get them through the lean time.

A sixty-six-year-old man who had a baby strapped to his back and had been the head of the village committee for thirty years (fifteen years ago) told me that some people used the money up as needed, and then, a year later, when it was time to repay the loan, they looked around for some way to drum up the money. For him, that meant selling one of his pigs (which had not been bought with the loan money): "We used the money to eat first, then to clothe ourselves. When it was time to repay, you have to prepare the money by selling a pig" (June 7, 9:30 a.m., field notes).

What he indicated was that planning for his future required taking into account immediate needs. At the end of the loan term, finding the money to repay was an immediate task, not too different from finding money for his needs. So although the microloan design intended that this "extra" money would be used for profit making, the borrowers' pressing daily needs, emergencies, or debts often had to come first.

"Microcredit ... Gives Us Money for School Tuition"

Studies of microfinance in Bangladesh and elsewhere have shown that funds there are not really being used for making money. Many times, they go toward housing or travel costs for migrant-worker family members, even though the bank has approved the money for things like rice-husking projects or other small-business activities.[6] Surveys in 1997 and 2000 show that in rural China, too, funds went to the agricultural tasks they were already doing (buying fertilizer, livestock) or else were consumed by daily expenditures, weddings and funerals, education, health care, or repayment of other loans.[7] That borrowers do not use the money for profit making is also obvious in the way that those who do repay get the money for it. A greater proportion of the repayment money is transferred from relatives than is earned in the borrower's business efforts.[8]

I spoke to a thirty-nine-year-old woman who had just finished washing her hair, which was wrapped up in a rag on her head. (While we spoke together sitting in her courtyard, a young woman listened in, and an elderly woman with a baby on her back wandered in to take a look at me, then walked back out.) My interviewee told me about using the money for needs when she got it and then finding a way to repay when the loan was due. But this didn't work out for everyone. She knew of people whose small group wanted to repay on a defaulter's behalf but couldn't come up with enough money among them. For her, microcredit was a good thing on balance because it offers money for school tuition:

> I didn't borrow from anyone in order to repay the loan. We went out to work (da gong) or else sold pigs and chickens in order to repay. I've heard of people who couldn't repay. Their small group couldn't help them. They didn't dislike the person, though, because he really *couldn't* repay ... Some people take out loans but can't repay. People need money for school tuition and other thing. ... Microcredit is good. It gives us money for school tuition.
>
> (June 7, 9:30 a.m., field notes)

As has been found in other studies, these loans were not an agent of poverty alleviation but rather a source of extra cash for the poor as they weathered life's storms.[9]

"We Are Too Poor ... To Try New Ideas"

As one twenty-eight-year-old woman with two children in tow told me, she and the others in the village do not have opportunities to try entrepreneurship. She knew some people who did make a little money from the loans, but others used the money for daily needs.

> We are too poor in this village – we have no ability to try new ideas for making money ... No, I haven't taken microcredit before. No kin of mine has, but others in the village have. Some made a little money, and some just used the money for daily uses (chi diaole) [literally, "ate the money"]. Some bought cows, pigs, sheep, and made money that way ... I'd do the microcredit if I could, definitely. What I would do with the money depends on how much I got. If it were 1,000 RMB, I'd buy a horse or cow. If it were 2,000 RMB, I'd do the same. If more, I might try to sell some small things, like candy.
>
> (June 9, 10:30 a.m., field notes)

She said she would do the microcredit if she could, but it was out of her reach. It wasn't that she didn't have any ideas but that she was "too poor." This was something that others indicated to me – that they wished they could take out the loans but could not afford to. What did it mean that they could not afford a loan for poverty alleviation?

"I Was Afraid I Wouldn't Be Able to Repay It"

Although microfinance is intended for the poorest people, many of the villagers did the math and knew that they would not be able to make the regular payments, so they opted not to take out a loan at all. As one forty-two-year-old woman told me, "No, I didn't get the microloan. I wanted it, but I was afraid that I wouldn't be able to repay it" (June 4, 2 p.m.). Another forty-five-year-old woman elaborated on the same thought:

> I haven't been taking microcredit loans. I did [before, but] it was difficult to repay. I think that kind of loan is good for people who do business, but not for us. If we buy a pig with the loan money, that pig hasn't grown yet by the time we have to make a repayment, and it is not good for us. We repaid without having to borrow, but there were people who did have to borrow. We want microcredit, but we are afraid we won't be able to repay.
>
> *(June 7, 10 a.m., field notes)*

Those who had miscalculated had to borrow from family and friends to make their repayments. A sixty-year-old woman told me, "Some people had trouble repaying, so they borrowed money from kin to repay. Everyone in the small group [of borrowers] had trouble and borrowed money" (June 3, 3 p.m., field notes).

"What's So Great About It?"

Several problems worked against the success of the microfinance program among the villagers: the loans offered to them were not large enough for the most beneficial projects; some villagers were too overwhelmed with the stresses of regular life to take on a new venture; and some had much more pressing needs, such as health care and education, that took priority over profit ventures. The money was nice for a while, but when the repayments started, ordinary villagers were left scrambling. On balance, the villagers did not feel that micro-loans brought much benefit. A fifty-two-year-old woman I talked to wasn't impressed with the Grameen replicator: "Some people had difficulties repaying and so borrowed from kin and friends in order to repay it. We did. We wanted to do it. But it wasn't so great. What's so great about it? We had to repay amounts twice a month. The payments were too frequent" (June 7, 9 a.m., field notes).

So, while some villagers raised extra livestock with the loan – using their own saved money (or hastily borrowed money) to make the frequent repayments for much of the lending period – most took out the loans because they could use the cash for daily needs. Microcredit was for them a means of deferment rather than investment. However, on balance, the loans were not a great help, as the interest payments were relatively large, and villagers could end up in more debt than they had avoided by deferring.

The social-collateral design of the Grameen program assumed that the loans would be desirable, so much so that borrowers would convince other borrowers to repay in order to acquire subsequent loans. As it turned out, the loans were not much of a benefit – many villagers refused to participate in the second round of the program – yet borrowers still repaid. To explain this outcome requires going beyond the immediate calculus of the individual and examining the status system in the countryside.

We are led to ask why the expectations of successful entrepreneurship were there in the first place. And how could the other assumptions inherent in the model have been so off-base?

UNIT OF ANALYSIS

Models of group-lending used the individual as the basic object of analysis, and this created the core dilemmas perceived by designers. Recall the aspects of personhood introduced in Chapter 2. The *unit* can be understood on a range from small to large. When someone refers to people, what is pictured? This might seem obvious to you if you picture various independent individuals. But for many on the planet, people aren't individuals, but rather clusters of interacting elements.[10] For others, picturing separate entities feels foreign, and individuals are understood as *parts*, as interacting fragments of a whole personality.[11] Closer to the middle of the spectrum would be the unit that is the exact size of one individual, who is not a *part* of anything but is himself an internally consistent whole. This is the popular unit of analysis in microfinance.

Following the individual-sized unit is the unit that is larger than the individual. Included in *his* analysis is his network, because he cannot be imagined apart from that which shapes him and through which he shapes others. The perspective of *guanxi*, American pragmatists, and relational sociology would fall here.[12] Finally, we have the very "large" unit of a person who actually encompasses all others, even existing as one and the same with the cosmos (suggested by the Hindu philosophy of "atman is Brahman").[13]

While important theoretical perspectives analyze the social world in units larger than the individual, global development focuses either on the *individual* or, alternatively, larger systemic forces surrounding him (more on this in Chapter 6). But ethnographic research challenges the supposition that the individual (in this case, the borrower) is the determinant of the outcome; it shows that a bigger unit is necessary, as the *relationship* between creditor and debtor often determines the outcome of real programs.

As an example of the significance of these relationships, consider how at the Grameen Bank in Bangladesh, when repayment problems were increasingly cropping up with male borrowers, the bank began shifting its loans to women, who were viewed as submissive, shy, passive, and immobile.[14] Bank officers were more successful in persuading them to attend weekly meetings and to make their loan repayments. Bank officers were also wielding control over the exclusion, inclusion, or replacement of borrowers within a group – even though the group members themselves were supposed to be deciding on the recruitment of new members. Other studies of microfinance in Bangladesh show that credit is a resource used in maintaining a one-sided power relationship; lenders are more like patrons than banking professionals, and "the structure of brokerage integrates access to formal development resources into networks of patronage."[15] One third-sector organization even took its microfinance borrowers to court in order to induce repayments when peer pressure failed.[16] This motivated, highly interactional move by the lender would never have come from Stiglitz's faceless, interchangeable bank (Chapter 2).

These ethnographic studies show that microfinance borrowers make their decisions in conjunction with the relationships that they have, sometimes as a result of their status or their location within a power structure. At the same time, other studies show that lenders also make *their* terms depending on their context. In other words, not only are the borrowers situated in relationships, but the lenders are as well. In Egypt, for example, some microfinance programs are part of efforts by multilateral institutions to forcefully support a power hierarchy, and this affects to whom they lend, how they set the terms, and the repayment outcome.[17] Imagining that microfinance outcomes depend upon the individual decision-maker as a self-enclosed unit – for whom calculations emanate from within – ignores the social and institutional context of both the lender and the borrower. Instead, we can look to *guanxi* to understand microfinance, which, as Kipnis describes, does not take the "rational, unitary, and non-contradictory Cartesian subject" as its starting point.[18]

When context goes unconsidered, we are assuming a situational blank slate – that there's nothing there of consequence before the development professionals arrive. Consider James Ferguson's observations of a development project in Lesotho in the 1960s, where development professionals were determined to promote livestock development.[19] Assuming that there was no semblance of organization before they got there, they began by fencing off the 32,800 hectares of cattle-grazing land into eight controlled grazing blocks to facilitate their plans. But there were already people there who were using the land, and they already had procedures, routines, and ideological disputes for its uses, privileges, and protections. They responded to this expensive (and offensive) effort by cutting the fences, knocking them down, stealing the gates, and burning down the office of the association manager.

THE RICH OF THE POOR

Like in any society, there is a pecking order even among the very poor. In the villages of rural China, at the top are the village cadres and the other influential villagers who can simply be described as people who have the ability to get other villagers to do things. Those with this informal but valuable clout include heads of clans (family groups), people well connected through intermarriage, and particularly charismatic individuals. Qualities that made one powerful in a village include agricultural knowledge, personal leadership skills, and large family-kinship networks. Such a person wasn't necessarily limited by the official terms of the microloan and might be able to borrow more money in order to get a truck or agricultural machinery, which has more and immediate profit potential.

Even this benefit must be kept in perspective, however. Trucks get a lot of use and might break down, and machinery only operates if there is electricity available. Still, for those influential villagers, the microfinance program operated quite differently from what has been described thus far. That's because in rural China, an asymmetrical flow of gifts and favors means that there is a steady stream of benefits that go "upward" to the more powerful.[20] In contrast to some parts of India, where the powerful reinforce inequalities between castes by giving gifts and so maintaining the indebtedness of their subordinates, ordinary villagers in rural China often provide services (if one has special technical skills, for example) to cadres and other influential villagers, in addition to giving them face by attending their ceremonies and presenting the customary gifts. In return, the ordinary villagers hope that the goodwill of the influential villagers will one day come in handy (when there are jobs to be assigned, for instance). The gifting also parallels the cultural pattern, where traditionally, people

give gifts to and serve the elderly (parents, older relatives) and authority figures such as teachers and leaders.

Georg Simmel wrote of "the unearned increment" or "surplus
value" of wealth: "The wealthy man enjoys advantages beyond the
enjoyment of what he can buy with his money."[21] In rural China,
those who are comparatively richer (though still don't have much by
global standards) are served more reliably than others and receive more
in gifts, favors, and other benefits. Microcredit – specifically, one's access
to microcredit – became one of those things that ordinary villagers gave
to influential ones, who were then able to collect multiple loans. Since a
small loan was not very helpful to an ordinary villager, it made sense to
"trade it in" for a boost of *guanxi* with an influential villager.

"Really Poor People Always Repaid"

So the influential villagers received larger loans, and their repayment
schedules were not as strictly enforced. Paradoxically, however, the
poorer people tended to repay, while the richer people did not. Large
proportions of these larger loans were never recovered, and they made
up the bulk of the unpaid funds. (That's why even though nearly all of
the villagers repaid, less than half of the money was actually returned.)
One assistant party secretary acknowledged that "Really poor people
always repaid, unless they were in a special situation, like someone
got sick or hurt," he told me. "Nonpaying people tended to be better
off" (November 7, 11 a.m., field notes). Although he knew he was
supposed to lend to the poor and not the rich, all of the administrators
lent to the richer people in exchange for their cooperation: From his
point of view, the administrators had a situation on their hands where
they did not have to worry about the ordinary villagers (since they
tended to repay), but they had trouble with the richer villagers, who
needed to be kept happy but tended to default.

A Failed Attempt to Collect

Township officials sometimes made efforts to remind influential villagers to repay, but these were largely ineffective. In one township, the

assistant mayor even tried to use *me* as a type of leverage to get a couple of influential villagers to repay their large loans. He wanted a certain young government official to help us, because the assistant mayor did not speak the local language of those two families. The trip did not pan out quite the way he had hoped, as the younger official was indisposed, and the two families seemed to have caught wind of our visit and were conveniently out. I recorded the events in my field notes:

> After we arrived in the government office, we had lunch, and then we had break time. I [did laundry] and retired to my room. [The assistant mayor] had told me that he would take me around to Mrs. Dan, who was in charge of microcredit and knows a lot about how it was done, as well as two families who didn't repay their loans, at 3 p.m. At 3 p.m., I went to the office, and [the assistant mayor] said he wanted Hong to take us, because he can speak [the dialect]. A guy came by and said that Hong was drunk. [The assistant mayor] said we'd go see if he was really drunk or just faking drunkenness. We went to Mrs. Dan's store/restaurant/house, and he was there, drunk in the bed in the kitchen, because he had had lunch there and then was drinking. Mrs. Dan wasn't there anyway, because her youngest son was taking the high school entrance exam in [town] these past few days. So [the assistant mayor] and I went by ourselves to a house a little up the hill where the family had borrowed 7,000 RMB plus interest, and had bought a truck with it (as [he] explained it, the previous year). The truck was overturned in an accident, and the owner was hurt, so they haven't repaid the money. But, now they've recovered financially from their losses and should pay it back, but still haven't paid it back. Their house was fairly nice, above average standards. Then we went back to the government office and, joined by a party official, went in search of another family that had not paid back their loan. We walked for a bit, then asked an old man where their house was, and he led us part of the way. When we got there, nobody was home, so then we just walked back. There were some

white, tiny "strawberries" in his field, so we picked some and ate them, then walked back.

(June 8, 3 p.m., field notes)

So I had become an unintended participant in this township official's failed attempt to recover two of the larger loans that had been taken as part of the microfinance program. One of the borrowers had taken out 7,000 RMB ($875), seven times the intended loan size! But what can be done to stimulate people to repay a social-collateral loan when they are already rich in social collateral? It was the assistant mayor who was actually poor in this asset. He didn't have rapport with the influential villagers. He was part of the township government and not a local. He did not even know the language. He needed the help of his staff, but he didn't have much pull over them – even those who were sober.

Besides, information traveled quickly; everyone knew we were on our way, and the defaulters left before we got there. There was no lack of information about the loans and the defaults that the influential villagers were involved in, but the availability of information did not mean that repayments were more likely to happen or that people would pressure one another successfully.

What the Books Showed

When I asked to see the accounting books for the Grameen-style microcredit programs, some officials showed them to me willingly, others seemed nervous, and one township refused my request entirely. The books I did view demonstrated the situation that staffers had already described to me: some money went to individuals in 1,000 RMB increments (organized into small groups), but sometimes a large amount was listed next to one name. Some of the books began with meticulous notation but broke off a month into the program, while others showed careful writing all the way through the one-year cycle. There was also variation in repayment rates: some segments showed 100 percent repayment, while others showed something nearer to 30 percent.

One illuminating visit was when I asked a GH staff member, Jane, if we could go look at the Grameen-replicator repayment records for the township she was in charge of. She made a phone call and then arranged for a driver, and we visited the building a few days later. In this township, the person who had been in charge of microfinance had already rotated out of the position. The official who showed us the books was nervous but forthcoming with explanations for the many discrepancies.

In this township, ordinary borrowers got 2,000 RMB (double the amount in other townships). But that was not the only unusual thing. They had a sort of "house rule" that people could give their loans to someone else. So someone who could convince others to give them their share of the loans was able to take out five loans, essentially, instead of one. And sometimes, it seems, even repaid funds never made it back to where they had come from.

> We (Jane and I, with the driver) went to Huangpu – on Friday, Nov. 4. We met up with the guy who had the microfinance records (a nervous, balding guy who combed his hair across the bald spot on his head). He actually brought his books right at the start, so I don't think he needed persuading, although he seemed nervous and kept apologizing and saying that the township didn't do the microfinance well (*zuode buhao*). He said that a lot of the loans were not repaid. The loans were administered using the rules that all the townships had – 1) lend to the poor, not the rich, 2) lend to the women, not the men, and 3) lend in small amounts, not big amounts. He also told us that at times, some of the small-group members would repay their amounts, but then the small-group leader they gave the money to didn't turn it in to the township – so it wasn't recorded. The guy who was in charge had left, though, for another place.
>
> We looked through the records and found what I was looking for, so Jane told me stuff while I entered it into Excel. Everything seemed normal (and the loans were pretty much paid) until we got

to the second loan cycle, where the records started getting strange. The guy told us that the records showed that one person would take out loans using the names of all five people in the small groups, and this happened with a large amount of the money in the second cycle. So they didn't go by the rule of loaning small amounts, not big amounts.

And a lot of the big loans were not repaid ... When one person took out the loans for an entire small group, that means the person took out 10,000 RMB, which is a much larger amount of money. That's when things weren't going so well – the people taking out the big loans didn't repay very much. Jane thinks that they are holding out, hoping that if they wait long enough, they can just keep the money (they know the guy in charge has been moved to another location, and they know the government isn't very strict about collecting the money).

(November 4, 9 a.m., field notes)

These trips to the township offices, and our perusal of the dusty microfinance accounting books (with pages and pages of handwritten records) had shown me that there was a big difference in the way that the loans were given out to different classes of villagers. One set of people had borrowed 1,000 (or 2,000) RMB and repaid every fifteen days. Another smaller set of villagers had borrowed much larger amounts, up to 10,000 RMB. If they were unable to repay their loans, or if they did not want to, the township officials had little recourse except to cajole them to pay the money back. (Other researchers have observed "loans" given out by the village cadres that everyone knows will never be repaid.)[22]

BENEFITS OF CONNECTION IN THE VILLAGES

It isn't just the influential villagers who benefit from the ethos of reciprocity in the village. They could use their influence to improve the lives of ordinary villagers as well. For instance, a cadre could have an ordinary villager listed as a member of an ethnic minority group, and preferential treatment for ethnic minorities has been policy since the 1980s. Among other benefits, minority students receive bonus points on the National Higher Education Entrance Examination when they apply to universities.

One man whose family seemed to be in perpetually difficult circumstances had not been accepted into a microfinance small group, because his neighbors considered him too big a risk. We had a conversation that was filled with awkward pauses, but the lines on his face indicated a smiley demeanor, and he was very, very polite:

> No, I haven't gotten microcredit. [He lowered his voice, speaking in a serious, pained tone.] I never have had any loans like that. Well, you know our family circumstance. We've never been able to get a loan. I wanted to get one, but when they were dividing up to form the small groups, where there are five families in the group, they said that they thought we wouldn't be able to repay the loan and refused to include us in the group. [It got really awkward because he was so pained and embarrassed, and Hong, the staffer, asked me where I am from in America. Near New York, I said. Then I asked the man, "How many children do you have?" to talk about something that is pleasant to him. Six children: one daughter, who is married, and five sons. The eldest son doesn't live in the village but moved away. I found out later that his son's wife couldn't get used to village life, so they moved to the city to live. We resumed the interview.] Yes, there have been big changes in the village. We eat much better now. [Again, to lighten the mood, I asked him what he needed to do today. He said he had to hoe – *wa di*, or dig the dirt.] We took a photo, and he offered some fruit.
>
> *(June 7, 3:30 p.m., field notes)*

He didn't have a TV, so he was not as rich as some of the others, but the staffer who was accompanying me told me that he's not especially poor, just a little below average. However, by his own explanation, he was, like others, "too poor" for microfinance. In this case, he had been excluded from the small groups, unlike the villagers who voluntarily eschewed the loans for fear of defaulting. But while he was not well off, even by the standards of his village, he had a good enough relationship with a cadre to gain himself an ethnic minority listing – a very valuable thing. Again, information about "wrong-doing" was not lacking among the villagers. Everyone knew about his falsified classification (which is how I learned about it), but that did not mean that they sanctioned him (unless there was something more behind the microfinance cold-shouldering, but that still wouldn't be outright sanctioning).

Other benefits that influential villagers can provide (especially cadres) include improvements for an entire village. Yan has noted that cadres have, since reform, increasingly played the role of the middle-man or mediator rather than enforcer of unpopular policies.[23] In fact, a cadre could also mastermind projects of huge importance to ordinary villagers. The difference between a proactive village head and a disin-terested one could be substantial to quality of life. Many of the villages in the site did not have electricity. As one thirty-five-year-old woman told me, "I have been living here for nineteen years. I was married into the village ... There is no electricity here, so there's nothing to do but chat. We don't dance together, but sometimes we sing songs" (June 9, 10 a.m., field notes).

But some villages did have electricity, and the difference could be the efforts of the influential villagers. I spoke to one thirty-eight-year-old man who had previously been the village head. He described how although the government had supplied the village with water ducts "as part of their poverty-alleviation program," he took the lead in mobilizing the villagers to obtain electricity. He gathered contribu-tions from everyone and led them in constructing the lines: "We brought electricity to this village – everybody contributed some money, and we did it ourselves. The government wouldn't do it for us" (June 8, 9 a.m., field notes).

Another time, I met a cadre at his home, which had been partly converted into a classroom for the children in the village. The village school, where his daughter was a teacher, did not have enough classroom space, so he had offered his home. This cadre, whose name was Yang, had been born in the village and had previously been the village head for eleven years. He was currently on the village committee.

So influential villagers could be seen sometimes as heroes, sometimes as villains, or most usually, something in between. While they did receive superior benefits, they also "gave back" to the masses in complex exchanges. Some of the influential villagers did things to benefit the villagers (whether within or outside of the law), and for that, it made sense to many villagers for them to get some special treatment. It would even make sense that when programs such as microfinance come along, some people would be willing to give their share of their loans to someone who had either helped them in the past or had the ability to help them in the future.

Though the microfinance program was not particularly helpful, ordinary villagers played along. The program benefited the influential villagers, and it was in the interest of ordinary villagers not to irritate them. Recall that the villagers considered loans as being made to families, not individuals. So where microfinance is concerned, cooperation with one important member of a family can mean cooperation in the future from an entire constellation of their relatives.

THE REPAYMENT TRIANGLE

Cadres, as influential villagers who were also working for the party-state for the time being, were able to relate well to the other villagers. But as we saw with the example of the assistant mayor above, the township officials were much more removed and did not necessarily have much control over villagers, especially influential ones. To the township officials, the microfinance program was another task to be accomplished in order to keep their jobs or ascend the power ladder. They received 40 RMB per month for their microfinance efforts, as a meager incentive to find a way to motivate villagers to participate. Their task was to get participation, keep the situation under control, stem any uprising or rebellion, and finally, demonstrate compliance to

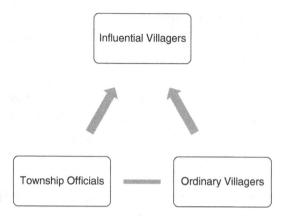

FIGURE 3.1 Power structure of the Grameen replicator

their superiors. For township officials, there was no need to demonstrate actual betterment of the village society, although that would be an extra advantage. Unlike the influential villagers – who lived in the villages and often worked to improve the area with efforts like bringing electricity and maintaining school buildings – township officials seemed more like outsiders. The easiest way to accomplish their goals was to make the influential villagers happy, which would gain their cooperation and harness the power of their influence among the village population.

The power situation was structured in the shape of a triangle (Figure 3.1). Everyone wanted to build up goodwill with the influential villagers. The township officials needed the influential villagers to support them. The ordinary villagers also needed to curry favor with the influential villagers, because having the influential villagers "on your side" could mean much smoother sailing through life. The influential villagers, of course, held everyone's attention and called most of the shots. Thus I call this situation the repayment triangle, with influential villagers at the pinnacle.

The Triangle Makes Her "Tired of Heart"

Li Ma is a township official, a representative of the Chinese Communist Party who works alongside the assistant mayor (the representative of the state). Her job includes preparing reports, reviewing applications for joining the party, and perhaps most importantly, enforcing state policies.

Li Ma treads lightly with her authority. Delicate village relationships and complex histories mean that she doesn't administer programs or execute laws haphazardly but rather with full attention to their consequences for influential villagers. Her goal is smooth implementation of policy, and if she alienates the large kinship groups in the villages, she will have trouble gaining their cooperation with the orders for which she is answerable. She is well aware that some of the mandates she is supposed to carry out don't make sense for the villagers and that enforcing them contradicts the realities of their lives, or even inflicts profound pain. For a while, forced abortions were dictated from above, but such very personal attacks on families and the family lineage were not taken well, to say the least.[24] My field notes record how miserable she felt being constantly surrounded by people who loathed her:

> She said that she feels like she chose the wrong profession – maybe being a teacher would have been better. She was afraid then of having so many pairs of eyes focused on her but now feels like she could do it. Being in the government makes her "tired of heart" (xin hen lei), because the villagers hate her and sometimes say mean things to her. And then there is a lot of drinking and hospitality that is necessary in the job, but that is something she doesn't like either. The last mayor of the township didn't like to drink, so he didn't tell the others to drink, but the one they have now thinks that people in the government should drink a bit.
>
> (June 8, 10 a.m., field notes)

For Li Ma, the stresses of her job come from her position in the middle. She is stuck between a rock and a hard place – between mandates from the party-state and the demands of villagers. Li Ma is an outsider here, having been assigned to this township. Her superiors further assigned her to work with Global Hope as a way to provide things that the villagers in the township need, including water and school programs. As township governments are given few resources, and taxing the destitute is an impractical option, GH programs are a welcome addition. Even though GH is there by permission of the party-state that employs Li Ma, when the GH county director (Little Wen) calls with requests, Li Ma carries out what is asked; it's part of her job.

"If Your Report Has Use, They Will See It"

Even when township officials were delicately balancing the points of the triangle – keeping the villagers provided for, the influential villagers content, and their jobs secure – action from above could cause their efforts to collapse. Yes, they are given a lot of leeway by the central government, and generally unchecked administrative power, but once in a while, quick and sudden strikes from higher levels bring panic and chaos. During the Hu-Wen administration (2002–2012), township officials were especially induced to follow mandates by the use of "hold-to-account" (*wenze*) tactics of selective sanction. Township officials who failed to carry out a duty to the satisfaction of those above were suddenly disciplined by lowering of rank, reduction of pay, a change of assignments, or removal from their positions. At high-profile moments, even leading officials such as party secretaries or government chiefs were targeted and forced to resign. (Top-down policy initiatives included protection of arable land, regulation of workplace safety, and regulation of excessive capital investment.)[25]

Microfinance fits into this climate as one of the things that officials are responsible to complete, generally with a lot of freedom. But, one never knows when there will be a strike. I explained earlier that some of townships let me peruse the microfinance records but one did not. The difference between transparency and resistance was, I found, whether the person who had been in charge of the loans was still around. I was there four years after most of the first round of

Grameen-replicator loans had been distributed. The programs were technically still running, because townships were still trying to get repayments, but many of the administrators in charge of the programs had now circulated to another official post. When, however, I visited a township where officials were still actively making loans, my request to see the records elicited an intense response.

The conversation had begun in an easy-going manner. The assistant party secretary was willing to talk about his work in the microfinance office, highlighting the lack of repayments before his arrival and his ability to collect 10 percent more than his predecessors had. But when I asked specifically to see microfinance records, he reacted with fear that the information would somehow get to those above him. He told me about a recent set of visitors from a university who had come without telling him and then had published a report about their observations online.

> There was a group of students and professors ... who came three months ago to research health and sanitation. They didn't ask permission, and we found them in the villages. They put their report online, and they didn't say where they went, but the people above us investigated every township because of that report. So now the people above us are very strict.

My efforts to reduce his worries only made him more anxious. He was sure that his superiors would see my report:

> I tried to say that my research won't be online and that there won't be any names or locations in it, but [he] started getting visibly upset, not letting me finish my sentences and raising his voice, saying that they would get in trouble. When I asked what they needed for me to see the records, [he] said I needed to go to the national government, then the county. I tried to say again that the people above him in the government won't be seeing my work.

At the end of that discussion, this assistant party secretary finally exclaimed that he wouldn't be persuaded:

"If your report has use, then they will see it. If your report has no use, then you wouldn't write it. So they will definitely see it!" Later, at lunch, I overheard his wife, who was also employed there, say to him, "I think you are overthinking this (*xiangde tai duo*) – it's not that big of a deal to let her see the records." To this, he retorted, "It would be fine if she saw them and didn't understand them, but she *will* understand them, and that will be a problem."

(November 7, 12 p.m., field notes)

This assistant party secretary was clearly fearful of being investigated by those above. Microfinance, along with the other things he was accountable for, was possible reason to be punished.

THE CHALLENGE OF CULTURE

In a Grameen replicator, the social-collateral design takes for granted that borrowers want the loans enough to convince other borrowers to repay in order to obtain more. It assumes that borrowers will channel their work into the free market and become entrepreneurs. It presupposes a financial stability that would allow borrowers to invest in something new. But the borrowers in this field site shared the kind of financial instability familiar to people who live in poverty all over the world. They were in a situation of highly variable cash flow, so rather than setting aside the funds for investment, they mixed their savings and borrowings, understandably using them to provide food and other requirements for survival in daily life. As for entrepreneurship, it was lacking. Some villagers had ideas that were slightly out of the ordinary (raise a cow, sell candy), but the limitations of the loans (small size, frequent repayments) precluded even these types of ventures.

The result of the Grameen replicator also depended, like any microfinance program, on the borrower-lender relationship. At this site, that relationship was embedded in a particular institutional history and social structure. The program was a top-down initiative in which the national government demanded certain results but, like with other directives, did not provide much oversight. These were the institutional features of rural China that the United Nations Development Programme report had noted would make it difficult to succeed with a Grameen-style program.[26]

Most borrowers repaid on time – even though the repayments were onerous and burdensome – because they did not have the power to defy township officials. Some ordinary villagers gave their share of the loan to influential villagers, who could then receive much larger amounts. And because they had enough informal clout for the township officials of the party-state to have to depend on them, influential villagers could keep delaying their repayments. Meanwhile, the ordinary borrowers who repaid on time were keeping the default rates low enough for township officials to get by. So people repaid for entirely different reasons than those depended upon by the Grameen program and predicted by Stiglitz's model. Rather than repaying so that they could receive another valuable loan, they repaid loans they didn't value much in order to invest in something priceless – their *guanxi*. This was especially true when it came to their relationships with the influential villagers.

The findings in the site show that predicting repayment outcomes is truly an exercise in frustration when one begins with the belief that it doesn't matter whom the lender is. (Recall Stiglitz's featureless institution – "bank" in one program and "government" the next.) In our case, the lender was the government, and that mattered immensely. The country's political history, the power structure of the Chinese countryside, and the way people cultivated their relationships made all the difference for who borrowed and who repaid. And local practical realities drastically shortchanged the hopes of program designers.

4 Repaying a Friend

What Makes Default Impossible

Yang, the cadre who had converted his home into a classroom for children (Chapter 3), had been elected guarantor for his administrative village's Global Hope (GH) microfinance program. As guarantor, he had agreed to repay – or gather the funds to repay – on behalf of anyone in the village who defaulted on the 1,000 RMB (plus interest) that was due after the one-year loan cycle.

Like the government's Grameen-replicator program, the guarantor program devised by GH was administered through the village committee. But the social-collateral mechanism this time hinged on personal ties with one elected villager, who, in addition to assisting with distribution and collection of funds, also agreed to personally guarantee the loans.

We began the interview by talking about reciprocity in daily life – the mutual help necessary for the daily tasks of agriculture and survival. Yang described the way people helped one another frequently:

> I was born here. I only know that my parents were here, but before them, I don't know ... There are forty-three families in this [natural] village ... We help each other a lot. I help you, you help me. We don't pay each other. When you need it, they help. We don't count how many times we've helped or think about whether we owe each other help. We help with planting. I help you one day, you help me one day. Kin and friends are the same. If you ask for help, they'll help. If a relative and a friend both ask for my help, I help the one who asked first. We dig irrigation canals together and fix roads together as a village. Weddings are by invitation. Funerals are also by invitation. But mostly all the people in the village are invited. There are some that are not invited. If [the hosts] are poor, they invite fewer people.

When we got to microfinance, Yang described how he and his two assistants interact with defaulters. At least according to this guarantor, defaulters were counseled but not necessarily sanctioned. And although a guarantor might offer money to a defaulting family member, others were treated in a way that was careful to save face:

> Yes, we have the [GH] loans. Only a few families don't. There are more than thirty families in this village with the loan. If someone has problems repaying, we figure out a solution (*xiang banfa gei ta huan*). We lend to the few who can't repay ... The three leaders talk to the people who are having trouble repaying. We don't offer to lend them money. Well, if they are kin, we might offer. You have to ask for yourself if you need to borrow money for the repayment.

When I asked the obvious (to me) question, "What happens if someone *doesn't* repay?" his answer was about logistics: ask the spouse to get the funds. When I asked, "What if both refuse?," he was shocked and surprised. That would be "impossible." The closest example he could muster up to what I was describing (default) was when a man had taken the loan and then left the village for good. But even in this case, his wife had repaid the money as soon as she could.

> If the husband doesn't promise to repay the money to the person who covers that family, then ask the wife.
>
> [Me: What if both refuse to promise to repay the money?]
>
> It's impossible that both husband and wife would refuse to repay the person who covers them for the GH loan!
>
> [Me: Really? Nobody has ever failed to repay someone in the village?]
>
> There was one family where the man went out [of the village] and didn't come back. So we repaid on their behalf, and later she [the wife] repaid us back. As soon as she had money, she repaid us.
>
> *(June 6, 9 a.m., field notes)*

So this particular kind of default – inter-villager – is not included in the universe of possible actions here. Reciprocity is such a moral norm (especially with something measurable like currency) that it was scandalous to suggest departure from it. This can be best understood when we keep in mind that social life in the village is done on what I call "the village stage" (more about this later in the chapter), and this stage is deep in the sense that actions performed there are *making* the person, not just reflecting his interior. What someone does *and* what is done to her *is* her identity, her face (hence "losing" and "gaining" face) in the eyes of self and everyone else around.[1] As I've emphasized so far, this aspect of self needs to be understood in order to accurately predict the decisions about repayment that emerge from the village context.

In what ways was this kind of default "impossible," and why? The response of the guarantor shows how, as people create their networks of relationships, they are creating themselves. It also confounds the expectation that repayment of a loan is unlikely without imposed interdependencies. The exchange of resources in the village has much to do with what it means to be able to hold one's head up, because a person creates his *guanxi* in part by maintaining his reputation in an interactive process of defining the self. The guarantor program positioned itself within the aspect of *guanxi* that makes people reciprocally obligated, where ethics are crucial and how well you treat your neighbor defines who you are.

DEFAULT, GUANXI, AND SEPARATION

Any serious discussion of default must take into account two important designations: what we consider to be an *economic transaction* and how we define a *person*. We know that a transaction is the outcome of individual calculations using information about circumstances (cost, product, demand, distribution), but it is also an offshoot of a relationship between the two transactors – in this case, the borrower and the lender.[2] So how we think about a person is just as important as how we think about their exchange of money.

It has been well understood that resources are exchanged through social relationships and networks, and that people understand money and credit in profoundly moral terms.[3] This is not surprising if, rather than being a preexisting entity who calculates internally and makes decisions by those means, a person is conceptualized as being "made," defined in part by the quality of his longstanding relationships with other people and his environment. And when one takes this view, overlooking morality in understanding and predicting actions would be irresponsible science.

If borrowing and lending is framed as an amoral contract between you and another person, then you could be assumed to have assessed all the information available to you and then made an agreement (the contract). Repayment means carrying out the contract, while default means reneging. If we understand borrowing and lending differently, however, not as a contract, but as an element of a relationship between two people who are being made on the village stage, we are peering through the lens of *guanxi*, and repayment takes on a bigger meaning. It is no longer your carrying out of a contract based on information you've gathered, but an announcement to the whole village about your relationship to the other person (and therefore about who you are). When it comes to the question of default in microfinance programs, it is possible that what is most important is what kind of person a defaulter would be perceived to be, and what value that person and others assign to that perception.

In the typology of personhood (see Chapter 2), the second aspect deals with how discrete the person is from other people and things, ranging from isolated to merged. Like the membrane that separates the interior of cells from the outside environment, how selective – how permeable – is the membrane that separates people from their social environments? This is what I call a person's *separation*. There are many ideas about how separate a person is from other people.[4] Most sociology is derived from the classical sociologists' assumption of a Cartesian model of the person, which relies upon high separation (more on this in Chapter 6). The American pragmatists were an exception, and work building on their challenge to the Cartesian model includes Charles Horton Cooley's concept of the looking-glass self.

Cooley suggests that one's self-perception grows out of interactions with others, as people shape their self-concepts based on how they imagine others perceive them.[5]

John Dewey also took issue with the assumption of high separation symbolized by the selfishness/altruism dichotomy. How strange it is, Dewey noted, to think of the individual as naturally isolated and becoming preoccupied with egoistic versus altruistic motivation. It is completely natural to be interested in "the welfare and integrity of the social groups of which we form a part."[6] He explained:

> The family, for example, is something other than one person, plus another, plus another. It is an enduring form of association in which members of the group stand from the beginning in relations to one another, and in which each member gets direction for his conduct by thinking of the whole group and his place in it, rather than by an adjustment of egoism and altruism.[7]

It is literally "nonsensical," Dewey asserted, to suppose that one's own interests are at odds with those of one's group, because "each one of us is a member of social groups," and the groups "have no existence apart from the selves who compose them."[8] Thus he found it bizarre to anticipate the selfish and applaud the altruistic (as if it were out of the ordinary). Kindness, he wrote, is unremarkable, since one is in a community: "The giving of a kindly hand to a human being in distress, to numbers caught in a common catastrophe, is such a natural thing that it should almost be too much a matter of course to need laudation as a virtue."[9]

Though people will deliberately try to improve their *guanxi* in the political arena, as described in Chapter 3, equally or perhaps even more important to people is the cultivation of *guanxi* in one's personal relationships. To be "a fully realized 'person' involves interacting properly with other people," explain Gold, Guthrie, and Wank.[10] Two key aspects of this full realization are reciprocity and the understanding and proper handling of people's emotional responses in social interactions. Morality and ethics do not emerge from the interior of an individual but are part of the individual's *relationships*. In *guanxi*, writes Wei-Ming Tu, a basic assumption is that "human beings come into existence through symbolic interchange," which is created only within social relations. The self is "a center of relationships," so there *is* no such person as an "ultimately autonomous being." Such a thing is unthinkable, since "the manifestation of the authentic self" is impossible "except in matrices of human converse."[11]

The assumption in microfinance models of a high separation of a person from others is challenged by the explanation of the "impossible default" in the field site. Similar to what has been observed elsewhere around the world, "interdependence" could never be "introduced" to these villagers by an intervention such as a microfinance program, as Besley and Coate suppose (see chapter 2). Interdependence is a baseline assumption of their lives. Important to *guanxi* cultivation are the actions (the giving of a gift, a friendly greeting) that express and build emotional ties.

That the basis of social relationships in the collateral structure matters is consistent with prior research: when researchers have introduced the opportunity for conversation between rounds of experimental games, they have found that even superficial discussion during these breaks influences subsequent decisions and outcomes.[12] If a few minutes of chatting among strangers can affect results, we can only guess how much real social relationships (imagine forty years of repeated "games" day in, day out) might make a difference. Concerted efforts to observe social ties at a development site might complicate planning, but their results could serve to advise the microfinance-program designers, to the benefit of their efforts.

MAKING THE PERSON ON THE VILLAGE STAGE

Erving Goffman characterized social life as theater, where a person is, in a sense, a joint enterprise: fronts are created, changed, protected, or cast aside during interpersonal interactions, depending on the audience's response.[13] These fronts are not external to the individual but rather props in the performance of the self, which *is* the self. Since the audience's reaction plays an important part in what happens in the performance, the self is not very separate from other people and is in essence made out of its interaction with the audience. For villagers in the guarantor program, repayment of or default on a debt has everything to do with their relationship to the lender and how they desire to be perceived as a person. Like seeing a reflection in a mirror, it takes no long deliberation for the borrower to see himself through the eyes of the lender (as well as the whole village); whether the borrower feels that people see him as a decent person happens instantaneously.

In anthropologist Xiaoyang Zhu's close study of a Chinese village, one of his interviewees, Guoyan, ran away from the village after gambling away borrowed money. The debt was only 200 RMB, but the money had been borrowed from his wife's brother. It was so shameful to have cheated his wife's relative that he could not bear to return. There was a story that circulated among the villagers: Guoyan's wife sometimes heard the sound of footsteps on her roof. It was Guoyan, people said, but she would tell her son to ignore the sounds. Everyone took the side of Guoyan's wife, saying that Guoyan needed to beg her pardon.[14]

In the field site, similarly, failure to repay a debt to a fellow villager – and worse, a relative – is considered a serious infringement. It complicates things further that people have known each other for decades in the villages and are in relationships that are not only long but also cross-cutting; due to very localized marriage, people often have relatives in several lineages.[15] For Guoyan, it meant that everyone knew not only him, but his wife and her relatives (the ones he owed money to), which has the effect of intensifying the ties. Everyone talks about everyone else's actions, so a good reputation can be someone's most valuable asset. Though it was another time and place, this dynamic is similar to what Robert Orsi found in studies of the residents of Italian Harlem in the early 1900s. People there were "made" in relation to other people (the family) and then judged and assessed (and further shaped) by everyone in the community. People demonstrated their honor, good character, good judgment, devotion to their parents, dedication, and ability to cultivate their relationships.[16]

Goffman shows the great extent to which interactions are intertwined with how we "make" our "selves," in the sense that who we think we are has a lot to do with how others treat us.[17] At the same time, there are some effects particular to this field site, including very close-knit communities.

CLOSE-KNIT COMMUNITIES

Personal ties within the sixteen administrative villages observed are quite strong by several measures: whether people know each other, the length of the relationships, and multiplexity. The men in the village had all been born and raised there, estimating that their families had been in the village for a mean of 4.5 generations, or about ninety years. The married women had come from nearby villages. The mean number of households per village was sixty-one. Villages ranged in population from 100 to 1,000, with a mean of 313.

With a group this size, everyone in each village knows everyone else by name. The shared history among the people who live there go back further than their own lifetimes, to the experiences of the family members of the generations before them. We could refer to sociologist James Coleman's concept of multiplexity and closure of social networks,[18] since people are linked to each other in multiple contexts, and all of the people in those contexts also know each other. Someone's neighbor might simultaneously be her aunt, her coworker during planting and harvesting season, a friend to chat with, someone with whom she has experienced meaningful events like weddings and funerals, and a source of wisdom.

Lateral relationships are very important to these villagers, as they have few bridges to resources outside of rural areas. Even if their children migrate to cities for work, these jobs are at the bottom rung of the ladder, not a source of political connections. Additionally, floods frequently wash out the roads in these areas, making social connections outside the village even more improbable and difficult to maintain.

The ability to access and utilize effective personal relationships is an invaluable resource in the shared struggle to maintain or improve one's livelihood.[19] The tasks of agricultural life, such as planting and harvesting – not to mention house building and maintenance – require working together. So does recovery from floods and other disasters. People realize how important the help of others is to their own survival, and so they cultivate their relationships just as carefully as they do their soil. There is also an intense social pressure to be known as a person who helps. Failure to help others in the village demonstrates a lack of *renqing* (human feeling), and failing to help a close relative is even worse. Such neglect speaks against one's very self, because "not loving those to whom one is bound by natural ties" is an extreme "of inhumanity," reports anthropologist Mayfair Yang. It leads to "ostracism by friends and relatives alike."[20]

Closely related to helping is paying back with mutual help. Expectations of people in daily life are shaped in rural China by metaphors of reciprocity (especially involving kin, such as debt to one's parents and ancestors). "Acting upon one's memory of past help is a central element of the notion of what it means to be a good or 'moral' person in many domains," writes anthropologist Ellen Oxfeld.[21]

Joint Conversations

In my first interview with a villager, I was introduced to what I would come to experience as normal – people considering interviews as group affairs, wandering in and out as they wished during the conversation. This excerpt from my field notes shows how there were no introductions to the various people coming in and out; they were not seen as necessary:

> Zhi and Ding took me to an office in the [township] government building for a bit, and I asked a few questions about the villages they were planning to take me to. Then we left and took a walk through the village center. While there, Zhi saw Xiong and took him with us. We walked from the center down a small, muddy road. Part of the way, we walked on a stone wall to avoid the mud. It might have been a fifteen-minute walk or so. Xiong was an older-looking man (forty to fifty) with a leathery, tanned face, wearing a blue

Communist jacket. We walked into his courtyard, where there were big branches laid out in bunches neatly. He invited us in (I glanced inside – mud floor, mud walls, a small fire in the fireplace, and no visible furniture), but Zhi and Ding said we'd rather sit outside. So they brought three tiny rectangular wooden stools for us to sit on, and Xiong squatted comfortably to talk. His wife was around, and presently his younger brother came to squat too. The children also hovered close by, and the brother's wife also sat with us, although a foot or so away.

(June 1, 9 a.m., field notes)

Xiong conveyed to me the kind of interconnected lives the villagers had. They lived together, worked together, celebrated births together, and cremated dead bodies and mourned together. But the way people behaved during his interview – displaying a joint owner-ship of the conversation – spoke as loudly as the actual content of his responses. People wandered in, sat down and listened, then left whenever they wanted to. Privacy was not a consideration.

Xiong told me that he had been born and raised in the village, and that before him, his family had been there for about 400 years. (Most of the families in the village had a similar history, though some had arrived as recently as five years prior.) It wasn't necessarily kin with whom he had the strongest everyday ties; it was neighbors who helped each other with the agricultural work:

There are six surnames in this village. [Xiong counted out each one on his fingers, with a certain relish.] We need roads, bathrooms – we should have at least one per family – and a cultural center. We play cards, mahjong, and dance together. We do our planting with each other, mostly our neighbors. Two or three families will work together to plant potatoes, corn, and some other crops. It's not kin who work together, it's neighbors, and they have different surnames. During a funeral, we help each other with the cremation, and with attending to the guests that come – the whole village helps with that.

(June 1, 9 a.m., field notes)

Reciprocal lateral relationships, including but certainly not limited to family ties, are an issue of great urgency in a place where institutional supports like publicly provided health care, emergency services, and infrastructure are undependable or nonexistent. Sometimes a favor granted can mean a significant quality-of-life upgrade, or even the difference between life and death. The "debt" owed in that case is great.

No Ambulance to Call

One afternoon, I was riding to a village when our car approached a man and his wife unloading crates. As we parked, the man greeted the driver of my car. Later, the driver told me that he didn't live far from the man who had greeted him. He also explained that this man felt obliged to him, because he had once found the man's wife unconscious and had driven her from the village, down the unpaved roads, and to the hospital in the town. This had saved her life. I recorded the conversation in my field notes:

> We drove a little bit down the road we came on, and saw a man and his wife bringing some soft drinks and bottled products into their small store. The man said hi to the driver, who told me later that he is quite indebted to him because, about two years ago, the driver took this man's wife to the hospital after she had attempted suicide by swallowing rat poison after the two of them had had a fight.
>
> (June 14, 1 p.m., field notes)

One can imagine that if this man owed the driver any money, he would certainly repay as soon as he could. But what's significant is that this was not a special, rare case. With no reliable government assistance, there were *many* opportunities for villagers to "rescue" each other out of one dire situation or another, and so they wore many hats, making their ties overlapping and quite strong. In addition to a neighbor as an ambulance driver, fellow villagers were also unofficial police, firefighters, plumbers, road-maintenance crews, and construction teams for house building. The only predictable thing about life in the villages is that you won't be able to make it alone.

Microloans Are Nothing New Here

Banking services are included in the things that people in the villages get from each other more often than from institutions. Education money is a common, recurring need. One man told me about the last loan he got from his friends and family, a group that included the township official (Little Du) who was accompanying me that day.[22] As he explained, he need only ask his friends and family for money, and he will receive it: "Yes, when I ask them for money, they will lend it to me. When my child was going to school, I borrowed money for the tuition. Kin and friends gave me the money I needed, even Little Du" (June 9, 12 p.m., field notes). This kind of monetary interdependence is not considered burdensome. Compared to the kind of collective life imposed during the socialist era, the villagers now can be said to be enjoying their financial freedom.

So borrowing, collecting, and repaying were already part of life in rural China, and not a unique innovation. The novel trait of micro-credit is that the repayments are organized according to formalized incentive structures.

A KINDER, GENTLER RECIPROCITY

Today's interdependence in the villages is much more relaxed since the end of the collective era. Deng Xiaoping's market reforms reestablished households as the unit of production, and new policies led to growing stratification and heterogeneity among former status equals.

One afternoon, I came across a group of eight older men and women sitting next to a few small tables with some things piled on top (some alcohol and what looked like small packages of food). They were waiting for a kind of traveling mini-exchange to happen; a truck would be coming by with things they could buy, carrying people who might buy their goods, too. They directed me to talk to a certain man, but as was the case with many of my other interviews, people interjected as they saw fit during my conversation with him. They told me about the differences between now and the collective era. During the collective era, the whole village would beat the person who didn't want to help, so in comparison, life now was less onerous, and people were happy with their freedom:

> They were selling some things and waiting for trucks to come by with people selling vegetables and other things so they could buy. They told me to talk to a man surnamed He, who was a man with leathery tanned skin, probably aged fifty to sixty, drinking white alcohol directly from the bottle. As we talked, he continuously drank from the bottle. And as we talked, the other older folk, mostly women, waiting in the circle interjected and answered my questions as well.
>
> [He:] "In the past, if someone didn't want to help with work that we should all do, the entire village would go to their door and demand that he come out and help. Now we have more freedom. If you can't go on a certain day, you can make up for it and go to help on another day. The village head doesn't fine you if you don't go."
> [A woman:] "In the past, they'd beat you if you didn't go help."
>
> *(June 1, 1 p.m., field notes)*

So, since the end of the 1970s, repayment and reciprocity in the villages has been less about avoiding suffering and more about fulfilling personal obligations. The older villagers had "the old days" as a direct comparison, but even the younger generations felt the shadow of that era. There was still a good deal of cooperation, whether it was in accidental circumstances or the regular course of events, but it was based more on relational ties.

One common need for working together in the villages is house building. It is not a matter of finding a contractor, agreeing on the terms of service, and writing a check. Instead, one invites people in the village to come help for the day. The custom varied; in some villages, everyone was invited, while in others, it was just kin and friends. Then, in appreciation for the help, the family whose house got built treated everyone to a meal. Later, that family would help to build other people's houses.

In an interview with me, a man surnamed Zeng went over which things were done in a mandatory collective way (digging wells, fixing major roads) and which were now the responsibility of people's own family and friends (building houses, digging irrigation canals). The former things were obligatory (though less viciously so than in the collective era), while the latter were dependent on one's own networks. But all the tasks relied on the other people in the village in one way or another. Like He above, Zeng expressed how they were enjoying the reduction of compulsory duties:

> As a whole village, we dig wells, fix roads together. When we build houses, we have friends and family help. We don't go do public work. There's very little public work to do. Digging irrigation canals is a private thing, because it's our own [fields]. Same with roads – they [smaller ones] belong to those few families that make it. I don't need to ask anyone for help, because we can do it on our own as a family. We do everything on our own ... Life is much better than it was before. I have two children who have grown up now and can earn their living. They are both teachers ... And I have one in college, and one more in the army. I have one granddaughter. The village has changed as a whole, too. Now we can plant our own crops, and do everything ourselves, not like during collectivization, when we had to do things together. I like it much better this way.
> *(June 7, 9 a.m., field notes)*

Interestingly, Zeng made what we might see at first as individualistic claims, but he considered a family (small group) working *together* equivalent to "not asking anyone for help" (and compared to the socialist past, it was). Doing "everything on our own" meant not a wholly independent effort but simply a smaller-sized group effort. In the shadow of years of compulsory collective activity, the villagers enjoy that their reciprocity now is largely voluntary, and that they have more choices in terms of whom they ask to help. This type of mutual help builds up their sustained relationships.

WHAT DEFAULT?

Statements made by the guarantors in the guarantor microfinance program must be understood in this context described above, rather than the figurative blank slate with no preexisting relationships, which is presumed in microfinance models. Their pledges to guarantee repayment for GH loans were not to them as much of a gamble as they might seem to outsiders; they were confident that they would be repaid. That's why being a guarantor was considered an honor (and perhaps a burden) but not really a risk.

One man, head of a large village and guarantor for GH loans there, belonged to a family whose lineage made up half of the village. Like Zeng, he also talked about how people help each other with building houses and are provided meals in gratitude. His criteria for choosing between two requests for help was based on the severity of the need:

> Yes, we help each other. We don't pay each other to help. If he helps you, you have to help him. [Me: If you help him five times, and he helps you two times, does he owe you three days of help?] No, we don't count how many times we help – we just help when it's needed. Kin and friends are the same. If a relative and a friend both come with requests for my help at the same time, I help the one with the more urgent need first.
>
> Our whole village helps to build houses together. The people don't get paid, but we give everyone a meal if they help. For one house, we need thirty people to help. We also participate in weddings and funerals as a village. For funerals, we need lots of people to dig a grave.

Regarding microfinance, his role as guarantor allowed him a certain power to help others, or as he puts it below, "fix the problem." He could petition GH for a payment extension for special circumstances, or he could arrange for his assistants and himself to cover the loan repayment for a period. In this way, guarantors act somewhat as mediators, communicating with GH (distributing and collecting the cash, asking for extensions) and coordinating within the village (working with borrowers, acting as substitute payer or appointing others to do so). In a context where everyone helps everyone from time to time, loan defaulters do not suffer shame. Since there is no lack of information among the villagers, everyone knows that the defaulters are using the money for something important, like a child's education. Besides, the borrowers are typically the poorer people in the town, as the loans are too small to interest the richer ones. And it isn't their fault if someone in the family gets sick.

> If someone can't repay the GH loans, they can come to me as the leader, and I can ask GH if they can postpone the repayment ...
>
> Twenty-two families have loans. Those with loans are all the poorer people in the village, because the richer ones have no need for the money. Last year, two ... families had problems repaying. We helped them fix the problem. The first family I repaid for, and they repaid me later. In the second family, someone got sick and couldn't farm their land, so they asked me to repay for them, too. Both have paid me back. Whether people have problems or not depends on whether it rains enough. These two families came to ask me for help – they are both kin. Four out of the twenty-two families with loans are my kin. The rest are my friends.
>
> The loans are useful for buying fertilizer for crops ...
>
> The three guarantors (*danbao ren*) who are elected do it as volunteer work. They elected us to communicate with GH, so we get the money from GH, bring it to the village, and then collect the repayments when the loan period is over. We have a meeting where people bring their repayments. I find out who has trouble with the repayment the day when they tell me. They don't lose face if they have trouble repaying, and it's ok if everyone knows. They don't feel bad about it, because maybe they have a child in school who uses 200–300 RMB per month. So they don't mind if others know; nobody thinks they are lazy.
>
> *(June 20, 9 a.m., field notes)*

Guarantors described their election as an honor, but it is also an obligation. And guarantors might themselves have to borrow from kin and friends to cover defaulters. Still, as explained by this other guarantor from another village, it is hard to refuse once nominated, although people may not say so overtly:

> There are thirty-three families in the microcredit program, 146 people total. It's all one group, so the three leaders are responsible for all of them, and if anybody doesn't repay, then the rest of the village gets no more loans. Ten days before the money is due, they [GH] notify the leaders, and we tell the villagers to prepare the money. The last round, three families couldn't repay, so I paid on their behalf – they took about three months to repay me, and it was 3,400 RMB.
>
> They chose me to be small group leader, which means they think I have the ability to repay. It does give me some pressure (*xinli you yali*). Few refuse if they are chosen – it is an honor, and if you refuse, people may not like you. The three leaders divide the money they are responsible for when they pay on behalf of the villagers.
>
> *(July 30, 1 p.m., field notes)*

Both the borrowers and guarantors show a high level of comfort with the person-to-person debt arrangement. There's no unusual risk in helping, and there's no shame in being helped. As a social-collateral structure, the guarantor loans fit right into the kinds of social relationships that people in the villages already have: they depend on one another, information is not lacking, and expectations for borrowing money from one another are clear. Most importantly, default is truly inconceivable. Everyone repays when they can.

"I Trusted the Borrower"

Some guarantors transferred the debt of defaulters onto themselves, but if guarantors were unable to personally provide the defaulted funds, they assigned other specific people – secondary guarantors, so to speak – to repay on behalf of those who were unable. Not only would these secondary guarantors lend the money when asked, but defaulting borrowers repaid the loans to their assigned lenders without fail within a few months. In effect, once the person-to-program debt was changed to a person-to-person one, the obligation was transferrable as necessary.

Wu was a thirty-four-year-old man who told me about his experience as a secondary guarantor. I talked to him in the fields, and his wife and child were nearby. His hands were covered in white dust from handling fertilizer. We talked first about a topic interesting to both of us: whether he would mediate between two fellow villagers if there were a threat of violence. He had a clear sequence of actions that he would take in the event of a conflict, because, as I learned, this is one of the things that villagers typically handle among themselves, apart from official entanglements. After talking directly with the person "who is doing wrong," Wu said, he would ask his kin to help, then the village head. If the issue was still not resolved, or if the offender seemed incorrigible, at that point he would approach the village committee.

> Yes, I'd mediate if somebody wanted to hurt someone else. I would go directly to that person. I haven't done so during the past few years, but I have done it before – it was one of my kinsmen. I talked to him, and then it was resolved. But even if it were not my kin, I would mediate. I'm not afraid of the possibility that they might yell at me too if I try to mediate. The one who is doing wrong is the one who must change. If he doesn't like it, then we have to educate him. If he doesn't listen, then there's nothing we can do about it.
>
> If I needed help resolving a problem, first I'd ask my kin, and then the village head, and then the village committee. I don't have different opinions than the leaders when they make their decisions about who is wrong and right in conflicts. If someone hurts me, I forgive him. I don't need to educate him. But if he were to hurt me repeatedly, like two or three times, I would not tolerate it. Then I would tell the leaders to educate him. First, I'd go to the village

leader. I wouldn't go and talk to [the offender] directly, because he has already done this three or four times. Doing it twice would be o.k.

I wouldn't say anything to him beforehand, before talking to the village leader.

Paying a loan on behalf of another borrower in the village was done in the context of all this – cooperation, working together, conflicts, forgiveness, fighting, resolutions, educating – in village life. These were not one-time contracts or deals but a part of a continual exchange and ongoing relationship that people had with one another. Two years prior, Wu told me, there had been one defaulter. Four or five borrowers, including himself, had been assigned to cover the defaulter, each giving 100–200 RMB. Although he was not sure how these assignments for secondary guarantors had been decided, he did not hesitate to chip in:

> Yes, we had GH loans. Last year, one family had problems repaying. We gave 100–200 RMB to cover that person. Then in the second year, that family borrowed 1,000 RMB to repay the people who helped him in the first year. Four or five families pitched in to cover one family. The three leaders decided on the people who were to give the loans to that family. I don't know how they decided it.
>
> [Me: Did you wish that they had chosen someone else instead of you to lend that person the money?] It affects the whole village, so I did it for the village.
>
> [Me: Was it fair, how they chose those who were to bring out their own money to cover that family?] [He fell silent, and there was a long pause.] I can't say. But I trusted the borrower.
>
> *(June 19, 2 p.m., field notes)*

For guarantors to agree to do the job – whether that entailed transferring the debt to themselves or assigning others to repay them – was a kind of cooperation, but it didn't have the characteristics that a contract implies. For this secondary guarantor, the basis of putting up his money for a fellow villager was not the fulfillment of a contract but rather a broader trust in the general pattern of interdependence (he had likely known this villager for a long time and exchanged mutual help with him): He was certain that he would be repaid. Fairness and unfairness about one particular loan weren't topics at the front of minds. To quote the guarantor discussed above, "We just help when it's needed."

"Our Village Has a Lot of Trust"

One thing that I could not tell from the fieldwork, however, was how likely it was that other villages are like the ones described by the guarantors I interviewed. Global Hope only implemented the guarantor program in an administrative village *if* a guarantor was elected and pledged his post. If nobody accepted the nomination, GH didn't go forward with the program. Their plan worked in a sense; GH had 100 percent repayment. But I couldn't compare the villages to see what made a difference in a guarantor village.

One of the guarantors and one secondary guarantor I talked to mentioned something, however, that might give some insight. They called it trust (*xinyong*). Most of the borrowers with the guarantor structure did not bring up "trust" in their explanations per se, but the concept was communicated in the assumption that repayment would happen. One guarantor emphasized the amount of trust in his village, and he linked it to a measure of simplicity that comes from a smaller group of people:

> Our village has lots of trust. We've always been like that. It's our habit. There are very few villages that are like us. We all know each other in our village, and when there is a wedding, the entire village goes. When we build houses, it just depends how much labor is needed and who is free. If you help once, that person will help you when you need it. I help you, you help me (*wo bang ni, ni bang wo*). There isn't just one strong leader in our village. I think we have a lot

of trust here because it's a small village and it's easy to govern – it's simple, not complicated like other, large villages.

(July 30, 1 p.m., field notes)

TRUST AND PROPRIETY ON THE VILLAGE STAGE

One of my informants spoke of *li* in relation to whether he would respond to break up a hypothetical fight among neighbors. *Li* could be used as a synonym for what is simply right. It encompasses courtesy, respect, attention to the situation of other people (particularly elders), deference to authority, a sense of mutuality, and an understanding of what is the best thing to do in a particular situation. It has been translated as propriety, decorum, rites, ceremony, courtesy, politeness, and civility.[23] If an offender wasn't understanding *li*, then that person couldn't be reasoned with: "Yes, I would say something if I saw someone about to hurt someone else. I'd try and help. Sometimes people will listen, sometimes not. If they don't understand propriety (*li*), then they won't listen, right?" (July 30, 1 p.m., field notes). And to quote Wu, above, "If he doesn't listen, then there's nothing we can do about it."

Upon *li* also turns one's reputation. People in the villages demand *li* of each other, and everyone watches whether someone behaves with *li* toward her parents and other people. Memories of any impropriety are long (lasting for months, years, decades, generations) and difficult to leave behind. If things aren't made right quickly, relational rifts can be constantly reinforced in daily interactions, until there is little chance for redemption. Gaining a bad reputation could mean that your children and grandchildren retain that ignoble standing.

"I've Always Been an Outsider"

Labels can stay with people over several generations. In Zhu's study, he recounts how the nickname for a man people called "Big Torch" (*da diantong*) was created and then stuck to his family. As an adolescent, the man had once carried a flashlight with him on his way to meet a girl in a field before sunset. Everyone found out and made fun of his intentions to sleep with the unmarried girl in the field after dark (hence the premeditated flashlight). Years later, villagers would still ask, "Why did you carry a flashlight to see the girl?" Now married with sons and daughters, his family members also took on the label "Big Torch." His children were called "Big Torch's sons and daughters," while his wife was called "Big Torch's wife."[24]

One interview with a thirty-five-year-old woman showed me in particular how interconnection among people in the village determined much of one's fate. She described herself as someone with no kin in the village and just a few friends. Because of the actions of others (her grandfather, her mother, and her mentally challenged uncle), she had felt like an outsider for as long as she could remember. She had inherited her uncle's land but also her family's bad name.

> I don't have any kin here. I have a few friends. I do help with funerals. Actually, I'm an outsider. People look down on me . . . I just have a few friends and neighbors, but I don't communicate with the rest of the village. I'm on good terms with the village head, though . . . I've been hurt a lot. I ignore them. I tolerate it. If I say something, but they don't listen, there's nothing I can do about it [breaks down, sobbing].
>
> My grandfather was a landlord, so when the Communist Party redistributed property, we were labeled as former bourgeoisie and were disliked. My mother's brother was mentally handicapped and had been married but then had divorced, because his wife left him. Because my uncle had no children, my mother had me go live with him as his daughter from the time I was very small, about two or three years old. I've always been an outsider, and no one defends me when I need it. I've grown up as my uncle's daughter, and now I've inherited his land. My husband and I live here.

The consequences of this outsider identity – and likely enmities that her grandfather or other family members created with people in the village – was a paralyzing loneliness, and also a certain measure of abuse. Having graves near one's house was considered bad luck – and this is not on the scale of a black cat across your path; it is something much bigger. In the village, the consequences of having a grave nearby were believed to range from mild sickness to financial ruin to death. Against her protests, however, the villagers buried someone behind her house anyway. She felt so sad about this, yet completely powerless:

> Recently, someone in this village died in a car accident, and people in the village wanted to bury him right behind my house. It's a bad thing for a grave and tomb to be so close to one's house, so I didn't want them to bury him there. I begged and pleaded that they not do it, but no one in the village stood up for me. They buried him there anyway. People are so bad to us. We have no friends in this village, and no family here either. My husband's family is all in another village. I've been living here for almost thirty years, but I have no one to defend me when I need help. I'm an outsider, and people look down on me. I don't communicate with most of the people in this village.
>
> *(June 15, 3 p.m., field notes)*

So one's identity on the village stage had important conse-quences. One's place in the social landscape of the village was a big part of life. Like wind and water slowly carving canyons out of rock, the cross-cutting relationships in the village created its landscape, shaped by decades of continuous interactions. The multiplex relations and multiple interconnections among people in the village were quite strong, shaping the outcomes of disputes. The woman, outcast from toddlerhood, couldn't do anything about the offenses toward her, because those who might sympathize with her would have a hard time going against their relatives. It would be disrespectful for some-one to side with an outcast over one's own relative.

"If They Don't, They ... Can't Hold Their Head Up"

In the villages, people were very afraid of the shame of losing face (*diulian*). This adulteration of one's sense of self could come from shrugging off work, breaking codes of *li*, or even (as seen above) the dishonorable actions of family members. It was clear that the villagers made their decisions while considering how their behavior would affect who they were as a person, as one fifty-five-year-old woman explained:

> The things we have to do is dig when the water turns the mud and rocks onto the road. People will all help do it on their own, without others forcing them, because everyone needs it to be done. They do it on their own because if they don't, they will be embarrassed and can't hold their head up in front of the others in the village. Others will look down on them.
> [Me: Is that the same as losing face (*diulian*)?] Yes.
> *(June 2, 3 p.m., field notes)*

Whether someone could hold her head up in front of others speaks something about who she is, about her identity as a decent person. One of the things decent people do is contribute their labor willingly when roads wash out in heavy rains. And although this is a kind of internally made decision, it is also about who these people are. In the same way, decent people in the villages repay their loans. And default on a debt to a fellow villager could affect a person's identity; it could become part of who he is as a person. The impact of default therefore is not only the embarrassment of a broken contract but the dismay of becoming someone a person is ashamed to be.

WHAT MAKES DEFAULT IMPOSSIBLE

In the guarantor microfinance program's social-collateral structure, repayment was made an obligation of the guarantors or of specific individuals assigned by the guarantors to cover for the defaulter. In this way, unpaid debt was no longer the responsibility of the township officials, and that made all the difference. This program was more effective in the social context of the village, because it removed the problems stemming from the interaction between the loans and the three strata of rural Chinese society. It avoided the repayment triangle completely: Government officials who were involved through their work with GH were not having to answer for repayment challenges, because the onus was now on the villagers to work it out among themselves. All this was accomplished by transforming lack of repayment into an "impossible" default: a debt obligation among villagers.

What confounds existing microfinance models is that this innovation did not entail any additional or overt peer pressure. People *always* repaid their personal debts to one another in the village. Even an influential villager (more likely to default in the other program) would not get away with failing to repay a personal debt to a well-respected fellow villager.

Knowing why villagers frame default as shameful is extremely helpful. Borrowing and lending is not a contract, where two individuals assess information, agree to terms, and can threaten legal action in the case of default. Borrowing in the villages was about relationships, about survival, and about the creation of self. First, defaulting doesn't make sense alongside a desire to thrive; it is a wrong done to someone with whom one has had a relationship for years – someone whose help will be needed in the future to bring in the harvest, drive a sick loved one to town, repair a damaged house, or dig the grave of a deceased parent. Interdependence was not "introduced" by either of the microfinance programs – it was already what people's lives were centered around. *Guanxi* defined borrowers' social relationships, in which proper friendship and family relationships were intertwined with giving and receiving material help.

Second, as people are continually "made" on the village stage, repayment as an action takes on significant meaning. Money is exchanged, yes. But it is the activity itself of exchanging that is worth all the money in the village – because it serves to define the person. For that reason, it would be so shameful to default that it seems like an impossibility to the villagers. Being a decent person was the most important "calculation" they made about default and repayment.

5 The Social Cost of Sanctions

Why Borrowers Avoided Making Others Lose Face

One sunny afternoon, after a long hike up to a village, I met a forty-three-year-old woman surnamed Zhang. One of the small-group leaders responsible for collecting repayment in the Grameen-replicator program, she told me that two families in her administrative village (but not her small group) did not repay their loans. She knew exactly who they were, but she had never confronted them. At first, she did not see the need to explain why. As the interview progressed, however, she was willing to explain to me what was obvious to her: if she were to speak to those two families directly about the repayment, she would cause them to have bad feelings toward her and would stir up the wrath of their kin:

> If I go ask about those two families, people will hate me. They will ask, "Have you eaten too much, and is that why you are trying to boss me around?" And not only will the two families dislike me, but all the kin of the two families will also hate me. I don't want people to hate me, so I don't ask.
>
> *(June 9, 2 p.m., field notes)*

We saw in Chapter 3 that in the Grameen replicator, the benefit of the loans to ordinary villagers was just so-so, since it was difficult to scrape together the repayments every two weeks even if the borrower had used the money for the profit-making activity of raising extra livestock. The ordinary villagers repaid anyway, because they needed to keep the influential villagers and township officials happy for the times when they would need a favor. In Chapter 4, we saw how repayment to a fellow villager was assumed because of the moral imperative of reciprocity. Even if payment was delayed, it would come eventually; the alternative was utterly disgraceful. So the villagers did not want future loans very badly (or at all), and they were repaying either because of their position in the status hierarchy or out of a sense of duty to a fellow villager. However, we see here that even *if* the Grameen-repli-cator loans had been something the ordinary villagers wanted, sanctions were so costly to apply that they likely would not have been used.

What follows is a four-part explication of what sanctions are like in the villages. First, the socialist era created a historical backdrop that causes people to be cautious with their statements. At the same time, the social reality of depending on one's neighbor means that one has to have a *very* good reason to lose an ally in the fight for daily survival. This chapter spends the most time on the third and fourth descriptions; villagers mostly take care of conflicts on their own, with the village committee being the last resort. And finally, a sanction is understood as part of an ongoing relationship, or *guanxi*, with another person rather than a one-time transaction, and how one acts in these relationships enters into the realm of one's own identity. A sanction gone wrong could mean losing face and losing who you are as a respectable person.

THE SOCIALIST PAST

Although each village has its own unique history, the brutal campaigns of the socialist era fostered conditions of intense conflict (personally experienced by the current generation of grandparents in the villages) that have led in some places to withdrawal from public life. Demoralized, people simply did what was necessary in order to survive. Every time you make a fuss, you risk the loss of goodwill you might need later on to weather some new policy, state decree, or aspect of the new economic environment.

Zhang's administrative village was made of eight natural villages (*zirancun*), clusters of households and kinship networks living near each other. She had not been born yet when collectivization of the farms first happened. When she was small, everyone was organized into work crews, and people were assigned jobs and awarded points for their efforts. They grew all their food together and in addition had to sell a portion to the state as well as pay a portion in tax (in kind or cash). Basic welfare during the Mao years was collective at the "brigade" (now administrative village) level, while the state started at the "commune" (now township) level. Zhang was a toddler when the Cultural Revolution began, a time of tension during "struggle session" meetings and work points.

She was twenty-six years old when economic reforms under Deng began, and the brigade was renamed the administrative village. Households were officially allowed to plant their own crops again, but cadres (members of the village committee) sometimes called together everybody from the administrative village to talk about changes to rules and regulations or to do some of the few tasks still done collectively (like fix major roads). Now, people are not interested in ideological or political battles. Whereas in the 1950s and 1960s, people talked of courage, heroism, generosity, and self-sacrifice, in the 1970s and 1980s, this shifted. For a while now, people have been practical in their goals, focusing on getting enough to eat and, feeling like they're at the bottom of the heap, trying to rise up in China's big society.[1]

Interdependence Makes Amiability Priceless

Sun was a forty-year-old man with a gentle demeanor, around his village, which had participated in both the Grameen-replicator program and the Global Hope program. Sun was a cadre as well as the guarantor for the village (though not all guarantors were cadres). It was his job was to collect the repayment, but an influential villager in the Grameen replicator did not repay, Sun recounted. Some people ventured to say something, but when the response was not cooperative, they dropped the subject. Afterwards, everyone treated the defaulters like nothing was amiss, because they did not want to have a bad relationship with them:

> Even their kin talked to them. They still wouldn't repay ... He did lose face. But everyone still talked to him, because they won't want to have a bad relationship with him. We all live together here in the

village, and we've all been here for a long time. In their hearts, they might be unhappy and angry about this, but they wouldn't show it to the family that didn't repay. The small group members talk to each other about it.

Sun directly compared the importance of the microfinance loans to the relationships (*guanxi*) among villagers. It was no contest; *guanxi* won. The loans were merely "a small matter" in comparison:

> But these loans are a small matter, not a big deal (*xiao shiqing*) and are not worth ruining relationships in the village for. The relationship is more important than the loans we miss out on. If I've been asking for them to repay for two years, and they still won't do it, I'll just stop. He would say to me, "I didn't take your money, so what are you upset about?" This is a small matter. People think differently – some think that they don't need to repay this loan ... Without the loans, we can get by. But if the *guanxi* is not good, then we can't get by (*buxing*).
>
> *(June 14, 11 a.m., field notes)*

The Grameen-replicator loans were a "small matter," unlike the guarantor loans, which were debts to each another. The term *guanxi* is used to describe many types of relationships – between spouses, kin, and friends, as well as networking relationships for mutual instrumental benefit. When *guanxi* is established between two people, they are able to ask favors of each other. Good *guanxi* does not require that repayment of a favor occur right away or in the same form, but people know that they will be recompensed in the form of a favor or a gift. Keeping yourself afloat in the administrative structure requires having good *guanxi* with influential people.

But, as we began to see in Chapter 4, there is also a sense that people's *guanxi*, the social relationships they have cultivated and the networks they are embedded in, says something about who they are, their identity and personhood. When the Grameen replicator crossed the paths of villagers who were consciously cultivating *guanxi*, the villagers incorporated microfinance into the "flow of gifts," services, and benefits that went upward to the influential villagers.[2] In the guarantor program, people always repaid others because of their personal *guanxi* – the ongoing reciprocity and genuine emotion generated by treating others well – and because they wanted to be good neighbors.

And one can imagine that these were wise moves. Endangering friendships was not a good idea, as villagers needed to maintain at least a cordial working relationship with everyone. Right around the corner could be another natural disaster. Definitely on the horizon was another harvest season, with little machinery available and only neighbors for volunteer farmhands.

REEXAMINING THE PERMANENT ACTOR

The significance of a person's actions in shaping their *guanxi* – and their very identity – made sanctions at the field site enormously costly and far riskier than loss of future income. This is related to the third aspect of personhood in the typology introduced in Chapter 2: *permanence*. It describes the extent to which a person is fixed or in flux. Like the other two aspects of personhood – unit and separation – there is a large range in how permanent a person is presumed to be.[3] If sanctioning a fellow borrower for defaulting causes a friend or neighbor to lose face, a borrower who is seen as still developing *who she is* would be expected to refrain from sanctions, since in doing so, she becomes a bad friend or neighbor.

The pragmatists offer a theory that can comprehend the field site. Dewey and James focused on the way that a person is constantly developing. James characterized consciousness as a stream, a changing flow of thoughts and experiences over time. One's "selective attention" becomes habituated; thus a person can be understood to be constructing a narrative of self "out of the flow of conscious experience."[4] Dewey wrote about the "growing, enlarging, liberated self" that "goes forth to meet new demands and occasions, and readapts and remakes itself in the process"; it is a "forming, moving" self.[5] As mentioned in Chapter 1, there is no such thing "as a fixed, ready-made, finished self," because it is "impossible," Dewey writes, "for the self to stand still; it is becoming, and becoming for the better or the worse."[6] This ability to choose who one becomes is the basis of Dewey's definition of freedom.[7]

In Chinese, the term for being a person (*zuoren*) is actually closer to the active "making" or the sense-of-change "doing" than the passive, motionless "being," so *being* a person is thought of as *becoming* something, *making* oneself. *Zuoren* therefore conveys something closer to the Southern Tswana way of talking about people, in the sense that one can say that someone "knows how to *zuoren*," implying that the individual has the potential to "do" personhood well.[8] (Or, someone might not "do" personhood well at all – but either way, we are not talking about "being" something permanently.)

To *zuoren* well means acting admirably and respectably in one's relationships. (In Zhu's study mentioned above, Guoyan's failure to repay his kin greatly demoted his identity because it ran contrary to *li*, which we have discussed.) With *zuoren*, you are, in a sense, in charge of *who you are*, not only what you do.

Since one's identity – whether one is a good person – is malleable, however, it is also susceptible to shock and injury from the outside, as anthropologists working in many societies have shown.[9] So assuming that there is no cost to sanctioning one's neighbors and peers – and that with certain kinds of information, a borrower can "force the peer to repay" (as Armendáriz and Morduch do in their model, described in Chapter 2) – overlooks a massive element in all social relationships: morality. In actual human experience, for the most part, we expect that when we do something profoundly evil, we change who we are as human beings. And sanctions in rural China could be considered this profound; tearing someone down while he is engaged in the making of himself is a serious action. Even in everyday life, most of us understand that when we punish or sanction someone, we will likely incur pushback, straining our relationships. Most people also feel that *forcing* peers to do anything by using information against them is unsavory at best and unethical at worst. People wonder as they deliberate whether to indulge their fantasies of revenge or punishment, *what kind of person would I become if I did that?*

Seeing a person as in flux rather than fundamentally unchanging has the effect of making that person's actions in microfinance more significant; not only are goods being exchanged, but a person is changing in response to their environment. In other words, the theoretical significance of a program designer viewing a person as less permanent – under construction, so to speak – is an increase in the designer's attention to moral considerations. And this is a good thing. In microfinance, decisions about repayment, default, and sanctions – especially concerning one's neighbors and peers – can be best understood in light of moral understandings.

Elsewhere, moral considerations of honor and shame have been observed to be important in microfinance. Anthropologist Lamia Karim highlights the way that female borrowers participating in microfinance in Bangladesh prioritize their moral and kinship obligations. But the bank manager, who understands microfinance as an amoral commercial venture, sees the female borrower as an "autonomous and rational female subject who freely makes choices in the market."[10] Women create themselves as "bearers of family honor," so lenders who use public shaming in this context heighten strife for the borrowers.[11]

Avoiding embarrassment is an enormous motivator in social life. Everyone wants to be honorable, whether that means showing one's independence or upholding the family legacy. In microfinance, then, the question to ask is what allows borrowers to be – or become – honorable people?

AVOIDING CONFLICT ESCALATION

In addition to the mutual reliance that makes villagers prioritize "small matters" below more looming ones, there is another big reason why they do not easily start fights: they generally have to finish them themselves. When there is a dispute in the villages, the official line of grievance is to go to the village head, then the village committee, then the township, and then, theoretically, up to the levels of the county, province, and central government. But although the villagers understood this sequence, they told me that problems are overwhelmingly solved by informal means before they even get to the village committee, because they feel like they will have a better outcome if they figure out solutions for themselves. Therefore, people try to negotiate with each other and come to their own solutions to matters like how to distribute limited water and how to divide inherited property. The sense is that going to the village committee means that one has already lost the battle; negotiations have failed.

Additionally, the legal system is operated as a part of the administrative system, so the people who are in charge of other matters (usually the village head, members of the village committee, and the party secretary) also preside over legal cases. The government is quite "local," in that the people in charge are familiar faces with whom one has decades of history (as opposed to nameless, faceless civil servants who work in a big building downtown).

When it comes to paying back microfinance loans, opinions of right and wrong are not clear cut, and disagreements are inevitable. With an uncertain government-villager relationship now transformed into an uncertain creditor-debtor relationship (in the Grameen-replicator program), borrowers held conflicting opinions about what the loan required of them. As explained by Sun, earlier, some borrowers considered the money a form of welfare. Others felt it wrong or dangerous not to repay. But against the backdrop of complexities such as land and water disputes, microfinance is not usually the priority item. You have to save your emotional and mental resources for the struggles that matter; you have to pick your battles. One man described it to me this way:

> Village matters are complicated. If you tell them nicely (*haohao de shuo*), they'll listen. There are family problems. There are problems between neighbors. These problems make people nervous. There are spouses fighting. There are land problems, where one person builds things on boundaries.

If you have problems otherwise or you are unhappy about something, people go to the village head. If a husband and wife have problems, or neighbors have problems with each other, they go to the village head. If the village head can't resolve the situation, they go to the village committee. Pretty much all the problems are solved by that point. There are problems regarding land. If a family divides, how to the divide the land is often a problem. This happens when brothers separate, or parents separate from their children. There is also fighting over water.

We had the government microcredit program in our village ... At this point, about two-thirds of the families who participated have not yet fully repaid. After they borrowed the money, they didn't have any plans for using it for development; they just used the money for daily needs. Then, when the time came to repay the money, they didn't have it. By now, the interest on those loans would add up to be as large as the loan itself. There were some people who didn't feel that they needed to repay a government loan. They signed a contract, though. Some could have repaid, but saw that others didn't repay, so they didn't either. Some thought it was a donation, a poverty-alleviation project like in the past. Of the ten or more families that didn't repay, they were all neighbors, so they communicated with each other.

Some others in the village thought that it wasn't good for those people not to repay, but they wouldn't say so to their face. They don't want to endanger their relationship. We try not to say anything negative. It's a habit of ours. We're always like that. We don't say anything bad in order to keep the relationship. You know in your heart what's bad, and that's good enough.

(June 15, 9 a.m., field notes)

The microfinance loans were not the foremost issue in the villagers' minds, and in the midst of all the other possible conflicts, it was not normally worthwhile to make a fuss about default, even if cash was on the line.

The Grievance Pagoda

The official justice system in rural China has been described as a "dispute pagoda," an adaptation of the heuristic device in the field of law and society of the "dispute pyramid."[12] In the pagoda shape, the steps up do not resemble a regular progression or pattern of succession; instead, the levels are mutually exclusive in that access to the next level up depends on *guanxi* connections at the current level. The grievance pagoda, then, has no clear path for settling matters in court. Climbing it means ascending a social and political as much as a legal structure, because in China, the legal system is fused to the rest of state bureaucracy. This increases the value of personal connections to township officials,[13] because when grievances are experienced, access to higher-level solutions only come if one has family connections to officeholders. Yunxiang Yan describes the case of a widow accused of stealing public trees. Two cadres attempted to confiscate a motorcycle from her family as a fine, resulting in an altercation. Then, there followed a series of back-and-forth efforts to punish one another that illustrates the ways that people draw on, maintain, and negotiate their social connections to resolve conflicts:

> A widow was suspected of stealing public trees. When two local policemen tried to confiscate a motorcycle from her family as a fine, a physical confrontation occurred between the two parties. The widow accused the policeman of beating her and threatened to use her personal connections in the county police department to punish the offenders. Although no one knew whether she had relatives in power or not, the local policemen decided not to risk offending higher authorities and encouraged the Xiajia village office to give the widow 50 yuan in compensation. The policemen did not, however, want to lose face in the village; and so two weeks later they detained the widow's son on a four-month-old charge of gambling, and asked the widow to pay a fine of 300 yuan to free her son. Everyone, including me, thought the widow was defeated when she paid

up; but, to the surprise of all, she went to the county seat and came back with a note from somebody in the county government requesting that the local police department return her money.[14]

Yan's description of the widow's case shows how conflicts that engage the official process are resolved not only based on laws, rules, or administrative procedures, but also on the social resources available to people in order to negotiate their outcomes.

Villagers, then, who are mostly only laterally connected, typically work on the lowest level necessary – working out grievances privately among parties/families or perhaps enlisting a village leader to help if the matter is grave. Often, the grievance is handled even lower – at the level of the individual, through what some villagers named "forgiveness," a learned passivity or "not caring." A person seen as wise and discerning can play a role in dispute management, too, serving as an informal but respected mediator – a "judge" who is more accessible than higher government and perhaps widely acknowledged as fair.

Everything Is Negotiable

Because of deep interconnectedness among village residents, small conflicts can quickly become large ones that involve entire families. In addition, conflict could lead to loss of face, which, if not handled delicately, could end up being more consequential than the original offense. Villagers expressed that handling matters quietly was a priority. But the necessary passivity could lead to frustration, as expressed by a fifty-two-year-old man whose family had been in the village for five generations:

> Everybody in the village does it [collective work]. Lots of people
> don't want to do it, though – there's nothing we can do about it.
> They may lose face, but they don't care. If they don't help, people
> don't like them as much. A long time ago, there were more people
> who wouldn't help. It's poor here, so the government can't monitor

or regulate us much, and people have too much freedom. Seven to ten families don't go each time we do public works, but there's nothing we can do about it. Among those people are my own kin and friends. It wouldn't matter if I said anything, because as soon as I say something, they will quarrel and disagree with me. Ten years ago, I said something, and they quarreled and disagreed with me, and so I stopped saying anything. Most of the other villagers don't say anything either, other than the village head.

(June 9, 12 p.m., field notes)

Note that "the village head" is in some ways exempt from the taboo of confrontation. As a cadre, the person holds a measure of authority not shared by ordinary villagers. Sometimes, this first level of the grievance pagoda (and more rarely, the second level, the village committee) is pursued by villagers, including the man just mentioned, who elaborated to me about the decade-old confrontation: "What happened was that their sheep came over and grazed my land. So then I told them to watch their sheep. Then they hit my son. So I reported this to the government, and then they fined that family 800 RMB. I only got 300 RMB, though."

The neighbor's sheep had grazed on his land, which could mean a significant loss. When interpersonal confrontation failed and turned violent, an appeal to the village committee brought satisfaction.

Or did it? The wronged party only got 300 RMB out of the 800 RMB that was ruled. Because the "government" is also quite "local" in the same way that ambulance, taxi, police, and construction are, everything is personal. And everything is negotiable. It is likely that the fine was applied to appease this man, but then the execution of the fine was done in a somewhat casual way so that the other family would not be too angry either. Loss of face happened but was kept at a manageable level all around.

Passivity, Then Creative Negotiation, Then the Pagoda

A sense of resignation accompanying lack of official recourse was evident in my conversation with one thirty-four-year-old woman and her husband, who had taken out a loan. In my field notes, I noted how her house had a curious protruding section. I found out later that to settle an inheritance dispute, two brothers had literally divided the house through the middle with a curtain made of reeds and then added the extra section. Villagers often told me that dividing inheritance was one of the main sources of conflict; the settlement of this situation is an example of a creative (yet visually haphazard) solution in an environment with little legal intervention available.

The woman acted in a way that I took for nervousness, her eyes darting back and forth. She was not as prosperous as some of her neighbors. When we went inside, there were piles of agricultural supplies, less neatly organized than in other houses. When I asked about the collective work of digging irrigation canals – what happens if people in the village fail to contribute their share of the work – her answer was that she didn't care. When I asked about water, she said something similar. She spoke like someone with no power:

> Some go to do the collective labor, and some don't. I don't care if they go or not. Every family is responsible for a section of the canal, but if one person doesn't do it, someone else will and be unhappy about it. But I don't care, even if I have to do more work. If someone doesn't go, we might all together tell the village head. We wouldn't tell the person directly, because he wouldn't listen, and he'd definitely be angry.
>
> No, I wouldn't mediate if I knew someone were going to hurt someone else. If it's not my business, I leave. If someone does something to hurt me, whatever (*wu suo wei*) – I'd walk away.
>
> [Someone asked, "What if someone takes your water?"] If I can't get water, I can't get water. Whatever.

The wife took care of the first part of the interview, but then she left, so her husband took over to talk about their loan repayment. They had been able to cover part of their repayment, but they borrowed from family and friends in order to repay the rest. I asked, hypothetically, whether he would go to pressure a defaulter in the village. He preferred to ask the village head to do it, but he said he might, along with some friends.

> If someone can't repay, they go to family and friends for loans. I borrowed from friends last year, and this year I'll probably have to do it again. I don't have to ask for the whole amount. If I borrowed 1,000 RMB from GH, I might have 800 RMB and need only 200 RMB more, which is not hard to get.
>
> [Me: Would you talk directly to a family that isn't planning to repay, if the leaders weren't going to do it?] I might bring some friends and go talk to him. It's better to ask the village head to do it or go with us.

I also asked whether if there were a problem in the village that a leader wasn't fixing like he should, he would try to choose a new leader to fix the problem or would try to fix the problem himself. There was some silence for a bit, as he had trouble answering. Finally, as in his answer about sanctioning, he settled on strength in numbers: "I would fix the problem with my friends" (June 20, 1:30 p.m., field notes).

Time and again, I heard villagers reinforce the value of handling something quietly (or just "letting it go") or if not that, thinking of some creative win-win solution, and then only after relational break-down, appealing to the lower levels of the grievance pagoda. Someone in another township told me about how she continues to avoid a confrontation with someone in her village who holds a nasty grudge against her:

> There is someone who spits at me when she sees me. She wanted to plant a tree near my land, but I didn't want her to, because the roots would reach into my land. We got into an argument, and now she hates me. I just let it go. I won't do anything to get revenge.
>
> *(June 16, 11 a.m., field notes)*

I thought this was an interesting dilemma and mentioned it in some of my subsequent interviews. In one conversation with a man who had been in village leadership for some time, I asked him how he would have dealt with it.

We began that conversation talking about collective work. He said that there isn't much that needs to be done these days, but it was understood that everyone ought to go. Still, shirked duties did not necessarily earn a direct confrontation. Subjecting his neighbor to that impoliteness was making a statement about that person's worth: that he deserved to be treated impolitely. Since this meant loss of face – a demotion in stature – it would be met with offense.

This village head had a general principle of forgiveness first, reasoning second, and third, trying to understand the other person's perspective. He also expressed a generous assumption about the offender's internal self-talk, presuming that social conscience would finally win out:

> There is almost no more collective work to be done besides digging irrigation canals. Everybody goes to help, because they all need water. They must go. If they don't go, it's o.k. too. Others are unhappy. People are not fined if they don't help. Mostly, people will go to the village head to complain. But in general, the people who don't go know that they should go, and they say to themselves, "If I don't go today, others are surely unhappy with me, so I must go next time." People wouldn't confront him directly because he would be angry. It's not polite to ask, "Why didn't you go?" If you already know why he didn't go, then you are close enough to him to ask – but then you would already know and you wouldn't need to ask anyway.
>
> [Me: If you want to know why he didn't go, could you ask a friend of his if you don't want to ask directly?] Yes, I could ask a good friend of his, though, if I want to know.
>
> If someone were to do something bad to me, I'd forgive him, or I'd reason with him and understand why he did it.

Regarding the situation with the tree roots and the spitting woman, this man responded to my query with some creative considerations and solutions if the tree had in fact been planted:

> The law is not clear on a problem like that. If there is a big problem like that, it's possible that the two families won't speak to each other. One way that this problem might be fixed is that if there are two or three families who would be affected by this tree's roots, they could give money to the person who planted the tree to dig the tree out. If the two or three families were to go dig the tree out themselves, they would be subject to the law.
>
> *(June 6, 10 a.m., field notes)*

Having been village head for some time, he was accustomed to thinking about ways to resolve conflicts. He considered the tree roots to be just part of the problem; the loss of communication between two families also mattered.

In addition to the village heads, who might come up with a solution that avoided a formal submission to the village committee, there are also people who serve as a kind of moral authority, elders whose opinions people respect and comply with. An aged man surnamed Chen is one such person. Everyone – including ordinary villagers, influential villagers, and township officials – listen to him. He was candid with me, telling about how conflicts can arise out of everything from drunken arguments over reciprocity to institutional fraud:

> I mediate between people all the time. [Me: Once or twice a week?] Yes. [Me: More than that? How many times per year?] Definitely ten or twenty times a year. They do listen to me. When one person borrows money from another and doesn't pay it back, the two may get into an argument if they've been drinking. Friends will fight, and kin too, for this reason. Sometimes the government gives seed or money or other things to the villages, but the village head doesn't

distribute these things to all who need it – then I go and talk to the village head, and he listens to me.

(June 3, 12 p.m., field notes)

The local township official who was with me was embarrassed to translate the comments about the village head into Mandarin for me, but I had gotten the gist and repeated to Chen what I thought he had said, to which he nodded. When I asked how many (natural) villages he mediates/offers wisdom for ("Just one village? Or more?"), he said, "More." I asked, "Four or five?" He said, "Yes." I asked, "Ten?" Chen and his wife were smiling, and he said, "Yes." I said, "Twenty?" Chen didn't answer, but the township official told me probably not – that's too big a distance for people to travel. I estimate, then, that Chen helps resolve conflicts at least across the entire township, a population of 10,000.

Interviews show that the norm concerning conflict in the village is for affected parties to pursue resolution on their own. Barring that, friends and family might be brought in for support. Finally, the village head could accomplish a lot through creative problem solving. The official channel (the village committee), through which grievances are supposed to be addressed according to government design, is really a last resort for the villagers. Taking your case to the committee wasn't necessarily any more empowering than seeking advice from the village head, mediating through a wise elder, or just letting it go, knowing in your heart that you are right. The official channels do not differ much in power from the informal settlements.

Sanctions in the microfinance programs must be envisioned to occur in this same realm. They are not applied carelessly; that kind of strain on a relationship would not be worth the "small matter" of a loan. This is not to say that sanctions aren't a part of everyday life in rural China! But people are very deliberate about them. A sanction is never a one-and-done event. The sanctioner is entering into a conflict that could conceivably burn for a very long time and involve a large number of people. There has to be a good reason – normally a deeply personal, painful reason – to light the wick. It can begin when someone loses face by being embarrassed, because at this point, the offense enters into the realm of morality and profound identity. So people's passivity in the area of sanctions is not just a matter of avoiding petty conflicts; it's avoiding a real mess that they might live to regret.

LOSING FACE AND PERSONAL IDENTITY

"If There's Revenge, Then It Will Go Back and Forth Forever"

Villagers described interpersonal conflicts in the village as longstanding and complex. A thirty-five-year-old man confided that someone did say something mean to him recently. But he would not reciprocate this time around; he sounded like someone who had either learned the hard way or at least seen the results of retaliation: "Yes, I've been hurt by someone else. Recently, someone said something mean to me. I didn't do anything to get revenge. If there's revenge, then it will go back and forth forever" (June 3, 3 p.m., field notes).

As Xiaoyang Zhu explains, people are used to reciprocal sanctions. Many kinds of things invite sanctions, including the absence of a greeting, failure to repay gifts or borrowed money, pointing out the wrongdoing of friends or family in front of others, and sexual deviance. If a receiver of a gift does not reciprocate, then the giver does not give him any more gifts, and others (who saw the unreturned kindness, figuratively speaking, on the village stage) do likewise.[15] Interactions are long-term, as an action today links people both to the chain of events in the past as well as the likely future. Like nicknames that last several decades and are even inheritable (such as Big Torch, described in Chapter 4), disputes could last for a very, very long time.

The longstanding conflict between Mo Han and Dong Fu in Zhu's study is an example of how verbal sanctions can spark decades of back-and-forth retaliation.[16] One day, Dong Fu mentioned in front of others that Mo Han's son had stolen Dong Fu's belongings. This was embarrassing for Mo Han, and he was hurt when Dong Fu told everyone about it. He felt that it violated the rule of *li* between friends, where keep embarrassing secrets in confidence. Several years later, Mo Han publicly called Dong Fu as a "small man" (*xiao ren*), a Confucian term for an immoral and petty man unworthy of respect. By doing so, Mo Han was invoking fellow villagers to pass judgment on Dong Fu for being a bad friend. In an effort to win back his friend, Dong Fu held banquets for Mo Han, where he publicly apologized in front of everyone in the village. So one careless remark necessitated years of friction, entailing both loss of reputation and financial resources for the one who committed the misstep, *not*, interestingly, for the father of the thief. Stealing is wrong, but losing face in the village is a blow to one's very humanity; therefore, intentionally making someone else lose face is reserved for serious issues. The value of the object stolen from Dong Fu did not warrant the nasty way he had made Mo Han lose face.

"Even If Someone Else Says Something … I'm Losing Face!"

Loss of face can be devastating, and it can come out of the blue, because it could result from what someone does to you, not only what you choose to do. Zhu's study described a despised man who likely suffered from a mental illness and would swear loudly at others with a barrage of insults. The insulted person would then feel like he was losing face because of being humiliated by such a despicable man.[17]

Loss of face could even come from simply knowing the person who is doing the shameful thing. One afternoon, I interviewed a couple who shared a love story: When the husband was courting the woman who is now his wife, he would knock on her door. If no one opened it, he would sit outside in front of the door all night, waiting until the morning. Now aged thirty-six and thirty, with an eight-year-old daughter, they spent forty-five minutes sitting and chatting with me. We began by talking about how many generations their families had been in the village – nineteen. People help each other quite a bit in the village, and people also generally go to do the collective labor; if

the village head asks, then it's mandatory. Shirking your duties brings
dishonor on more than yourself, as the husband expressed:

> Yes, just say the word and we'll go to help with the collective labor.
> Sometimes it's five people, two people, or ten people. You have to
> go – you must, if the village head asks. The village head decides how
> many people are needed. You can't say, "I don't want to go." You can
> say, "I have something else I must do, but I will help next time."
>
> If you say you don't want to go, you will definitely lose face. Of
> course you would lose face! Even if someone else says something
> like that, I'll feel like I'm losing face, because it's that bad!
>
> *(June 14, 11 a.m., field notes)*

When someone does something appalling, everyone cringes a
bit. There is a bit of a collective breach of trust as everyone wonders
what else could happen, now that someone has defied shared practices
of how to be a good friend, neighbor, or person.

"I Wouldn't Want to Make That Person Lose Face by Asking for the Repayment"

Erving Goffman, writing on embarrassment, discusses the phenomenon of making someone else lose face. People don't like to feel
embarrassed, because appearing flustered is considered evidence of
weakness, inferiority, and defeat, so a tactful person will avoid placing
others in this position. They might pretend not to see that the person
has lost composure, or pretend that nothing is amiss at all. By doing so,
they protect the other person against loss of face, making it easier for
him to pull himself together. Failure to pretend for the other person,
though, results in embarrassment for everybody.[18]

Observations similar to Goffman's were expressed to me by the
Chinese villagers. They did not want to make people lose face, because
that's almost as bad as being the one who is losing face. A decent
person covers for your embarrassment, an indecent person fails to do
so, and only a brute would *cause* the embarrassment for an insignif-
icant reason. If you are the village head, and it is your duty to help

someone, then you might have the proper entrée into someone's business. But an ordinary villager would just be causing loss of face and maybe starting a lifelong feud.

A Global Hope staff person who was accompanying me told me between interviews that she could completely understand this perspective: "I wouldn't want to make that person lose face by asking for the repayment," she said (June 14, 11 a.m., field notes).

Because sanctioning in microfinance models has always been considered something where only the defaulter was shamed, it was surprising to me at first to hear that the sanctioner could also suffer shame for her actions. And since microfinance models only focus on the wrongdoing of the defaulter, there is no room for considering the sanction as its own moral wrong. But once I began to put it all together, it made perfect sense. If a neighbor (someone who is not kin, *very* close friend, or in a position of authority) pointedly asks a defaulter, "Why didn't you repay?" this subjects the defaulter to a kind of rude scrutiny coming from a peer. If the interaction is felt to be disrespectful, it could cut at the heart of one's very identity and therefore lead to a long string of retaliatory actions. But the embarrassment of the defaulter is precisely what the microfinance design is depending upon! All at once, it hit me: the success of the Grameen-replicator group lending depends in large part on something happening that everyone in the field site is spending a great deal of energy trying to avoid. The most intense depth of feeling came out in the interviews not with the topic of natural disasters, grueling daily labor, or lack of access to financing, but rather the making and maintaining of oneself as a person through avoiding embarrassment.

Are borrowers going to sanction in the way that microfinance designers are hoping? The question now seems simplistic. The answer at this site, at least for the Grameen-replicator program, is mostly no – because of the political-social history and the institutional context. Informal negotiations resolve most conflicts in the villages, people do not enter into conflicts lightly, and making someone lose face is usually unwise but also means something about you as a moral person.

6   Pragmatism and the Sociology of Development

The Grameen-replicator microfinance projects that I observed in rural China ended about five years after they had started. In three of the four townships I studied, there were no longer new loans being given, though administrators were still trying to collect repayments. When I went to look at records in one township, the administrator unlocked a door marked "Office of Microfinance," wiping away dust and rummaging through clutter for the account books. New microfinance projects still pop up in China and around the world – though now more often with the modest aims of providing a bit of cash for rough times or "financial inclusion" rather than the dream of eradicating poverty or enacting a development miracle. Microfinance maintains a presence in big institutions like the World Bank and policy schools, but interest in it is not growing.

By many accounts, the Grameen-replicator program in rural China turned out to be a dud. It proceeded largely unaware of its own premises and then quietly failed. Borrowers initially appreciated having a little extra cash to spend on education and health care, but the repayments quickly became burdensome. Yet someone *could* have written a report about this program according to typical measures – like money spent, loans disbursed, and even loans repaid – that wouldn't actually sound too bad according to industry norms. The report could be efficiently filed away, and meanwhile, the next cycle of funding starts and the process roils on. Repayment rates by themselves would have obscured what really was occurring in the program.

As for GH's guarantor program, it was doing a lot right. Besides the prudent alterations to the social collateral structure, the repayment period had been extended from two weeks to eight months so that borrowers had time to raise and sell livestock before any money was due. Yet even though repayment rates were very high, the GH staff expressed doubts after four years with the model. Borrowers did not appear to be much better off, and it was costing the staff a great deal of time and resources to distribute and collect the loan money. They were in the process of closing down the programs to focus on other, more impactful efforts.

Which aspects of the Grameen Bank's recipe for group lending were validated in this site? The recipe (Chapter 1) is as follows:

Small Loan + Poor Individuals + Group Repayment Incentive = Self-Regenerating Entrepreneurship

Both programs I observed provided a small loan to poor individuals along with a group repayment incentive, but neither led to self-regenerating entrepreneurship. The Grameen replicator's group repayment incentive led to a paradoxical outcome: Ordinary villagers did not benefit financially from the loans, yet they repaid on time. Or, they gave their share of credit to influential villagers, so they could get much larger loans (sometimes seven to ten times the regular size) and very accommodating repayment periods. But the economic environment was such that there was no profit to be made, even for those who used the loans to purchase trucks or large machines. The guarantor program gave the small loan to poor individuals with a well-designed group repayment incentive, but the dream of self-regenerating entrepreneurship still did not happen.

I've admitted that I began this venture by asking the wrong questions: whether the group-lending model had simply been administered badly or whether the events occurred because social networks "got in the way." But I found that the "people factor" wasn't peripheral; it was decisive. Group lending relies on social relationships and sanctions, which happen in the realm of what people consider decent, proper, trustworthy, dishonorable, shameful, and blameworthy. Whereas the predominant models of microfinance predict that people borrow and repay money without considering their relationship to the lender, that they sanction people they know without expectation of pushback, and that they use information to force their neighbors to do what they want, this book explains why these assumptions do not make sense for people in the field site (and may also not make sense elsewhere).

MICROFINANCE AND MAINTAINING SOCIAL TIES

While microfinance enabled some people to use their relationships to gain access to money (as the models emphasized), there were many ways in which it was the other way around: borrowers used the money and credit from the microfinance programs to maintain or develop their relationships. The pragmatist theory of microfinance (Chapter 1) was a better predictor than the other models: Borrowers repaid when doing so strengthened important relationships and when it made them a good person, and they avoided sanctioning peers when doing so incurred a social and moral cost.

Whether through the shame of applying inappropriate sanctions or the embarrassment of defaulting, microfinance transactions based on sanctions have potential long-term costs to relationships that far outweigh the cash value of the microloans. Additionally, *who one is* is often at stake. The risk to one's sense of self makes these "micro" loans not trivial at all but much more consequential than their small amounts might indicate. Being an honorable and good person can be of great import to the borrowers. This insight helps to explain reports of microfinance–related suicides, including that of a forty-five-year-old woman in India who hanged herself after she defaulted on four microloans amounting to $840.[1]

Microfinance, like the economy, is a cultural product.[2] Specific expectations of human behavior are embedded in its group lending structures, yet many felt sure that these were universal. As Julian Go observes, social theories that dress themselves up as universal are more often than not provincial, bearing the imprint of the "worldview, interests, and concerns of the socially dominant, hence of a very tiny if not miniscule group of people."[3] One contribution of *Borrowing Together* has been to single out one element in this construct – assumptions about what a person is – and to evaluate its role in the microfinance models. In order to summarize what has been learned along these lines, we revisit the three aspects of personhood.

Unit

Whereas group-lending models make the individual-as-entrepreneur the main unit of analysis, I found that to understand the Grameen replicator required an investigation of how borrowers cultivated their social ties in relation to status and survival. Lenders, too, lent the money so as to enhance the relationships they deemed vital. Microfinance intersected and interacted with borrowers' relationships with the lender, people in their social hierarchies, administration, and power structure, as well as personal ties.[4] Findings in Chapter 3 show how the configuration of social status in the field site – a power triangle of sorts where both the ordinary villagers and the township officials were trying to please the influential villagers, though for different reasons – led indirectly to the unexpected outcomes. What occurred was no longer only between the borrower and the lender: Ordinary villagers often signed over their loans to influential villagers (a third point on the triangle). (As the influential villagers could drag out their timelines indefinitely, these larger loans tended toward default.) The majority of borrowers (the ordinary villagers), however, scraped together repayments according to schedule, despite not making money from the loan.

Table 6.1 summarizes some of the social factors that predict repayment and sanctions in group-lending microfinance. The findings suggest the importance of what Jocelyn Viterna calls the "micro-processes" – the interactions between individuals involved.[5]

Separation

The sense that people are self-enclosed individual units with very little information about other people is reflected in the preoccupations of prominent models of group lending: shirking on the one hand, and informational asymmetry on the other. If high walls separate an individual from the "outside" world of other people, the internal workings of other people's motivations are unfathomable. So to combat the

Table 6.1 *Social factors in group lending that predict repayment and sanctions*

Borrower Actions	Social Factors
Repayment	• differences in status between borrowers • history between the borrower and lender • administrative and organizational structure of the lender • third-party social relationships affected by repayment or default • definitions of goodness and neighborliness
Sanctions	• reliance on neighbors for survival (agricultural, medical, transportation) • official (government-run) channels to redress grievances • informal processes for conflict resolution • social acceptability of embarrassing someone in different circumstances

envisaged problem of insufficient information, group meetings made sense to theorists. And since people are so profoundly separated, no one can know what peers might do, so there is always the worry of the free rider. This fieldwork suggests, in contrast, that borrowers are not fundamentally separate from one another, and that they define themselves by the way they behave toward their neighbors (including what they do in microfinance).

Borrowers repaid when doing so made them a good friend or neighbor. Borrower decision-making (to repay or default) was not always happening as program designers imagined; it was more instinctual. As Chapter 4 shows, borrowers in the guarantor program did not go through a cost-benefit analysis of the pros and cons of repaying or defaulting; rather, with immediacy and being attuned toward being a good neighbor, the borrowers saw it as "impossible" to default on a loan to a fellow villager. Rather than obsessing over potentially defaulting neighbors, the borrowers in the guarantor program were confident that their neighbors would repay. Information was never lacking about who was planning to do what. This analysis underscores the explanatory power for development sociology of instantaneous meanings that particular actions convey about a relationship.[6]

Permanence

While models posited that borrowers would use information to force their neighbors to repay to counter this problem, the findings show that borrowers do not easily sanction people they know, including friends, neighbors, and family. If borrowers do not want to be the type of people who embarrass others, they will not inflict sanctions in the context of microfinance. Predictions of peer sanctioning therefore depends on the circumstances in which embarrassing someone is acceptable and unacceptable.

Borrowers in rural China directed their microfinance behavior toward the type of person they wanted to be. Being a morally good person was crucial to how borrowers did (or rather, did not) apply peer sanctions: Borrowers avoided sanctioning peers when embarrassing someone incurred a moral cost. We must ask, "What allows borrowers to be or become honorable people?" and conversely, "What is considered shameful among the borrowers?" An understanding of the circumstances in which embarrassing someone is acceptable and unacceptable should help to predict whether borrowers will sanction. When embarrassing someone makes one not a good person, microfinance borrowers will not inflict the sanctions. Whether a borrower wields sanctions depends on what kind of person they believe they would become if they inflicted peer pressure or sanctions on a neighbor. Also important here is that social relationships constitute the self, and these relationships are reinforced, maintained, strengthened, or diminished with each interpersonal interaction. Therefore, people change over time as their relationships change, since their histories are shared histories, intertwined with other people. Neighbors and friends did not apply peer pressure willy-nilly; instead, they carefully considered the consequences of their actions on their relationships.

PERSONHOOD AND THE SOCIOLOGY OF DEVELOPMENT

This study has tested models of group lending designed by economists (Joseph Stiglitz, Timothy Besley, Stephen Coate, Beatriz Armendáriz, and Jonathan Morduch), but there are implications for development researchers more broadly. The theoretical basis for much social science research, including sociology of development, can be traced to eighteenth- and nineteenth-century European social thinkers, and is limited by the concept of personhood that social science research has prioritized. Some research focuses on the individual; others on systems containing the individual. Human well-being is said to improve, on the one hand, by the increase of individual freedoms and rights, and, on the other hand, by the decrease of structural causes of poverty and inequality. The social sciences, presuming of a sizable gap between the individual and society, largely define the outcomes of development in terms of political and economic benefits to individuals. Below, I discuss these approaches in an effort to articulate what is missing from current efforts to study global development.

Individual Capability

One position in the sociology of development falls within or is compatible with the Human Capability Approach (HCA; also called the Human Development Approach). Serving as the basis of the United Nations Development Programme, it is currently the most influential perspective – the gold standard that became the status quo – in development research. Mahbub ul Haq, Paul Streeten, and Richard Jolly, among others, created it in the 1980s and 1990s to expand the idea of human well-being beyond the narrow definition of income per capita. One of its key accomplishments has been the creation of the Human Development Index (HDI), a composite measure of life expectancy, education, and income that allows for cross-national comparison.[7] Two famous proponents of the HCA, broadly speaking, are economist and Nobel laureate Amartya Sen and legal philosopher Martha Nussbaum.

Sen's approach focuses on *capability* and *functioning*. Capabilities are the attainable options that individuals have, based on their skills and powers. This is the set of possible paths that a person could follow. Functionings are what people do, defined in terms of utility (feelings of satisfaction, the fulfillment of preferences, or the presence of choices) or of goods/commodities used. Following the HCA, development efforts seek to maximize individual realization of capabilities and functionings. Nussbaum's related project seeks to identify a list of fundamental capabilities that all human beings should be able to possess.[8]

Development ethicist Des Gasper observes that Sen's understanding of "capabilities" and "functionings" is a counterpart to the mental model in microeconomics, where individuals exchange *things* that can be given or taken away as commodities.[9] Seeing society as an assemblage of individuals who possess things (in this case, capabilities and functionings) mirrors Adam Smith's view of society as a free market where individuals have things to use and exchange.

I would say that both Sen's and Nussbaum's approaches conjure a picture of a person as an individual that has some things but not others.[10] A person ought to be in possession of certain attributes (like life span and health), abilities (to think, experience emotions, plan, and play), and control (over one's body and property).

As philosopher Henry Richardson has pointed out, this definition of human life is based on what he or she can do ("capabilities"). It implies that the disabled cannot live a good life, as they cannot fulfill the basic requirements of being a person, defined as having the capability to do a certain set of things; they are dependent on other people and in many cases cannot make their own choices.[11] There is the fiction embedded here that dependency – due to inability – is somehow unnatural or antithetical to real humanity. Because independence and capability *are* what makes people human in this view, dependence and inability are antithetical to being truly human.

A second fiction found in the approach is that people can "take or leave" relationships. It's their choice. This approach does *include* social relationships – they are subsumed under the capabilities umbrella, one of the things people may choose to do. But this idea that people can choose to have relationships if they want to, that relating to other people is one of the many choices people have, ignores the way that people create themselves in interaction with other people (unless, granted, you were literally raised by wolves).

Systemic Change

Another approach to the sociology of development has the same central concern – the problem of diminished individual autonomy – but focuses instead on describing how power and oppressive forces in institutions and systems constrain individuals. Within this approach, one camp hopes to build upon the virtues of existing structures; the other would be more likely to work to overthrow the structures because of their flaws.

The first group builds on Max Weber's work on institutions, working toward social mobilization and countering detrimental state practices and globalization processes. Although Weber saw the rationalization of modern life, in the end, as a coercive force upon individuals, his analysis highlighted the power of modern organizational structures (specifically, bureaucracy).[12] Building on Weber's analyses, a hefty literature asks what kinds of organizational structures and state interventions generate outcomes of economic growth.[13] Other questions are centered on private property, entrepreneurship, democracy, and other potential contributors to development.[14]

Karl Marx's theories of alienation provide the theoretical basis for the second camp. Marx saw capitalism as a vast economic system that oppresses individuals via their alienation from the goods they produce, the process of work, fellow humans, and even themselves.[15] Analyses stemming from Marx's work evaluate existing structures as systems of domination, examining the historical relationships between nation-states and pointing to increasing inequality as a result of the global capitalist system.[16] Their research traces the mechanisms by which rich nation-states and multinational corporations exploit poor countries and poor people. The body of critical literature on imperialism and post-colonialism that draws on Michel Foucault's work shows the different ways that power is imposed on people around the world.

Presumed Gap between Individual and Society

Adam Smith, Max Weber, Karl Marx, and their European peers in the emergence of social science in its present form all communicated a substantial chasm existing between the individual and society, and most explanations in the social sciences today depend upon this implicit gap. Subjects are measured and analyzed either at the level of the individual unit or at the level of society. René Descartes's philosophical statement, "I think, therefore I am," conveys that sense, shared with other thinkers as social science began to emerge, of the fixed individual separated from others. Robert Wuthnow observes the aspects of Descartes's philosophy that classical sociologists have espoused:

> [There is] a tendency to regard the human condition in terms of a basic split between subject and object. This tendency is in a sense a reflection of the Cartesian dualism that penetrated the thinking of all the classical writers and provided the distinctive epistemological outlook on which their work was based. At the heart of this dualistic conception of reality was the idea of a gulf between the self, as subject, and the external world, as object. The self, acting chiefly in the Cartesian view as a thinking entity, was aware of itself and of the surrounding environment but felt cut off from this environment.[17]

As reality is split into internal (subjective, private) and external (objective, public) realms, the way that individuals form through interactions with others is missing as social relationships are placed in the realm of the internal. They are part of the individual, her emotions and her internal state, and are seen as separate from the external conditions of social structure, such as GDP per capita, education level, political structures, and other objective avenues of development. Thus Descartes's assumption of dualism is alive and well in the presumed assumption in global development that problems can be solved by increasing individual freedoms, either by increasing individual competencies or by reducing the constraints imposed by structures of the larger system.

Pragmatism and Development

While most sociology is derived from the classical sociologists' assumption of a Cartesian model of the person, the exceptions are the American pragmatists – notably John Dewey, Charles Sanders Peirce, and William James – who were working out a competing notion of the person at the same time that classical sociologists were writing theirs. Pragmatism besieged Cartesian constructions of the person by arguing against the assumption of the predefined unit of the individual (where the self exists prior to the interaction, and thought is grounded in self-consciousness).[18] Their theories focused on how decisions emerge from interaction, and how people develop and grow. Below, I suggest three (wild) new directions for the sociology of development, given pragmatist critiques of social theory.

1. Poverty as the Absence of Good Relationships. Not only is the idea of the autonomous individual an unverified article of faith, but it also leads to a limited notion of the good society as one where individuals are merely protected from encroachments of his neighbor.[19]

We might take the cue from the villagers in this study. In cultivating their social ties (*guanxi*), they saw their own well-being in terms of the "richness" in relationships, not only their individual wealth. A counterpart for development sociology would be to define human well-being in the same way. Poverty, in the view of *guanxi*, is both the absence of good relationships intrinsically important to human beings and having bad relationships. This point of view contrasts with the view of development as economic growth and the more recent views of development as "freedoms."

Although global development research has focused either on things we ought to *possess* (capabilities) or structures that constrain people, pragmatist theory suggests that we imagine a research agenda beginning with a different answer to the question, "What is human experience really about?" Varying definitions of well-being are being increasingly discussed (one of these, for instance, is Bhutan's Gross National Happiness Index). Research in psychiatry, psychology, and sociology point to the importance of human relationships – in particular, parent-child and sibling relationships – as utterly vital to human well-being.[20] Satisfying relationships with family, friends, and romantic partners make lives meaningful and are, according to many, necessary for "a good life."

Because it distinguished itself by departing from the Cartesian model of personhood in the social sciences, pragmatist thought poses some fascinating possibilities for challenging the status quo in development research and opening up new avenues for research and policy. It could be possible to have an alternative notion of a good life as *one with good relationships*, rather than a life that is merely free from external constraints. What if we define a good society by the quality and quantity of good social relationships? Building on pragmatist notions of a person, the good life, and the good society, it is possible to envisage a sociology of development that is concerned not only with understanding structural constraints upon individual abilities, but also the contexts where good social relationships are possible.

Making social relationships a more central object of inquiry could inadvertently lead to a new way to turn its subjects into what anthropologist Arturo Escobar has described as "spectacles"[21] of development by mapping, rating, and judging those relationships. Yet it would seem to be almost irresponsible social science to disregard the vast amount of evidence that good human experience revolves around good social relationships.

2. Hidden Models of Commodity Exchange. Pragmatist theory is useful for exposing the hidden models that stem from the influence of Cartesian personhood in development research. There is a great deal of potential for sociologists to investigate the practical effects of the

Cartesian point of view on global development, including the disproportionate interest in self-reliance that is consistent with a view of people as highly separated, following Ann Swidler and Susan Cotts Watkins's study of the "sustainability doctrine" in volunteer-based programs for AIDS in Malawi.[22]

The underlying mental model of commodity exchange permeates language about even the most unlikely of things. As mentioned earlier, the Capability Approach treats abilities as if they were individual possessions. Pragmatist theory shows how ubiquitous this mental model is. John Dewey points out how strange is the tendency to speak of abstract things – such as hunger, kindness, or mercy – as if they were items outside of our bodies or otherwise separate from us:

> We may say, if we please, that he is moved by hunger. But in face hunger is only a name for the tendency to move toward the appropriation of food. To create an entity out of this active relation of the self to objects, and then to treat this abstraction as if it were the cause of seeking food is sheer confusion. The case is no different when we say that a man is moved by kindness, or mercy, or cruelty, or malice. These things are not independent powers which stir to action. They are designations of the kind of active union or integration which exists between the self and a class of objects ... Benevolence or cruelty is not something which a man *has*, as he may have dollars in his pocket-book; it is something which he *is*; and since his being is active, these qualities are *modes* of *activity*, not forces which produce action.[23]

Hunger (as well as benevolence and cruelty) absolutely are not things we "have," Dewey argues, they *are* us. The assumption of separation also pervades the language of research. While the sociology of development is steeped in language about highly separate units (whether framing the interaction as exchange or oppression), we will have difficulty comprehending human experience.

For example, Ferguson observes that development experts who value individual autonomy and self-sufficiency find it disturbing in today's South Africa when people pursue, even seek out, a subordinate and dependent status.[24] Dependence seems sad, even shameful, because in modern liberal common sense, society is composed of transactions among autonomous individuals. However, many around the world don't regard personhood as preceding relations but instead see themselves as constituted *by* those relations. Social personhood depends on your relationships, without which you are nobody.[25] If research begins with the premise that independence is better than dependence, the sociology of development will be irrelevant to big portions of the world's population.

3. Culture and Morality: The Importance of Becoming. With its emphasis on how people create themselves, pragmatist theory makes it possible to investigate morality, previously understood as internal and therefore inscrutable. When a person is understood to have "beliefs" located completely internally, the processes leading up to action are a complete mystery. Culture is difficult to examine when theory is limited to individual and systemic explanations, but seeing people as constantly *becoming* rather than fixed entities, adapting and remaking themselves as they make choices in relation to other people and their situations leads to a sociology of development with a core interest in culture.[26]

People create themselves in reference to shared understandings about good and bad, wrong and right – all facets of culture. Suddenly, what makes people rejoice – as well as what makes them mortified – as they engage in interchange with those around them becomes important and central objects of sociological inquiry rather than peripheral or pesky features. Like people elsewhere – as in Margaret Frye's examination of schoolgirls in Malawi and Iddo Tavory's study of an Orthodox community in Los Angeles – the borrowers were fashioning their present selves to become someone they desired to be.[27] Focusing what people aim to be (intertwined with the shared considerations about what is good and what is not) provides an account of moral work in the mundane and material realms of physical survival and making money.

REPAYMENT DATA, THE THIRD SECTOR, AND GOVERNMENT

In line with Wendy Wolford's observations about "the difference ethnography can make"[28] in development studies, this study uncovered what happened in the Grameen replicator in a situation where repayment data by itself would have told very little about the actual interaction between the ordinary and influential villagers.

If I had gathered just the repayment data, then I would have used variables such as "government" versus "third sector," I would have had results similar to other studies of microfinance in China, concluding that government programs have low repayment rates while third-sector organizations produce high ones. But this would confirm the validity of a false dichotomy between government and third sector. While there are differences when a third-sector organization participates in programs (often improvements), they cannot carry out programs independently of the government. Third-sector organizations can be successful even under these conditions (as detailed in Chapter 2): in this field site, third-sector organization's stellar guarantor program (by repayment standards – 100 percent) was not carried out separately from the government but rather, because of the constraints presented by the institutional context, in cooperation *with* the government's administrative structure, to considerable success (described in Chapter 4). Some of the same government employees who administered the central government's Grameen replicator also had a substantial hand in administering the Global Hope program.

*

The attempts to have people borrow "together" in hopes of alleviating poverty and advancing economic development did not quite work as expected; social relationships (*guanxi*) challenged the state-of-the-art accepted conventions about group lending. Borrowers repaid when repayment strengthened important relationships (lenders lent with the same aims) and when doing so made them a good person. Borrowers also avoided sanctioning peers when embarrassing someone incurred a moral cost. The main thing that people did with the microfinance loans was not to purchase equipment or other things for a profitable venture. Instead, the loans were part of the "equipment," so to speak, that people used to cultivate their social ties. Repaying a loan is, at the same time, also part of how a person builds a sense of self. In microfinance, people *do* access money through social networks, but they also do the opposite: cultivate their social relationships by moving money.

Appendix: Fieldwork Methodology

In this appendix, I describe the way that I gathered five types of data over three years: "go-alongs" with Global Hope (GH) staff, interviews, ethnographic observation, microfinance repayment records, and internal reports of the third-sector organization.

Before describing it in more detail, I share two big regrets about my fieldwork. The first is that my data on the villagers are derived from interviews rather than ethnography. The ethnographic portion of the fieldwork was with GH staff and government officials, with whom I lived, ate, shopped, cooked, walked, and worked, but these richer data were cut from this book once I decided to focus on microfinance and not the workings of a third sector organization in rural China. The data on how microfinance relates to the way villagers cultivate their social ties would have been much richer had they been based on direct observations. I wanted to spend more time in the villages, but as a friend of GH, it did not seem prudent to ask for this. I was sensitive to the precarious status of all third-sector organizations in China, and I did not want to burden that GH staff any further. Though I cannot be certain, I think now, on hindsight, that if I had tried harder, I may have been able to find a township official who would let me stay longer in the villages. My second regret is that I have had to keep so much information out of this book. The uncertain standing of GH as a third-sector organization and the unpredictable political landscape make it so that publishing a record of a failed government program presents a danger for those involved. So, I do not disclose the real name of Global Hope, geographic information, or year in which events occurred. Under other circumstances, sharing this information would allow for better analysis and discussion.

During the first segment of my fieldwork, I lived in a hostel in an urban area for thirty-two days, volunteering every day for thirty days at the GH office in that city. During that time, I acclimated myself to the work of the third-sector organization, and they got used to me. I accompanied staff on seven visits (a total of twenty-one hours) to clients and potential clients in their places of business, which included shop stalls, noodle stands, and a pig farm outside the city that we got to via a one-hour bike ride. I attended a meeting that twenty-six borrowers participated in. At the request of the GH regional director of operations, I conducted a survey of clients about their social capital; I surveyed forty-one clients during three meetings and presented eleven tables in a thirty-two-page report for the center. The regional director was pleased with the report; he invited me to dinner at his home with his family to discuss it. During this month, I had lunch with GH staff twenty times, and dinner with the staff twice.

If I wanted to eventually get to the villagers, I needed to leave the city. So I also spent the month visiting and gathering information about potential field sites. I considered four rural sites in total: two GH sites and two sites of other third-sector organizations. Of the four sites, one stood out as the most securely established, with stable relations to state officials. I chose this site because I needed to see a program in action and to increase my chances of gaining access to villagers (in a sensitive situation, outsiders are less likely to be granted entrée). The site I chose was a cluster of four townships, each composed of administrative villages. (They are called "administrative villages" because they are demarcated by the government, not necessarily by natural settlement patterns.) Each township had a population between 5,000 and 10,000. The four townships housed a total of sixteen administrative villages.

The next step was for me to begin operating out of the county seat that oversaw the townships I had chosen for gathering my data. So I moved to there, via a sixteen-hour bus ride, and arrived at the countywide GH headquarters. I met with the GH director at the county level, and she was very accommodating. A Chinese national who had taken a position with GH, she directed a team of both GH staffers and government employees who had been assigned to her. She introduced me to all her staff and then appointed someone to help me with logistics. She only asked that in exchange for the staff's participation, I provide her with the results of my research when I was finished.

While in the county seat, I lived in GH's living quarters, which were set up to accommodate staff from other offices, interns (university students), and the translators, consultants, and researchers who sometimes visited for a few weeks or months at a time. The quarters were about a ten-minute walk from the GH office. Also in our building lived Elder Brother Wan and his wife and son. (The people in the area use titles of endearment to address one another, especially if they are friends or kin. A typical nickname was a preface of "Elder Brother" [dage] or "Little" [xiao] before one's surname. Thus the staff called me either "Little Hsu" [Xiao Xu] or, if they had studied English, "Becky.") Elder Brother Wan was one of the government officials who had been assigned to work with GH. Though on the payroll of the government, his duties were to help direct GH projects, and he blended pretty seamlessly into the GH environment. At the county seat and at the township-government levels, GH staffers and Chinese government officials worked together, and this integration of government and third-sector was not odd. The staffers were employed by GH, and the officials were employed by the government, but they acted like one crew. Everyone answered to the GH director. At the township level, the lower-ranking government workers who had been assigned to help GH also assisted the local township mayor and assistant mayor in their projects.

While in the county seat, I first shared a room for seven days with a young Chinese woman who was there for the summer as part of a university internship. Then I shared a room for five days with a GH staff member who had been with GH for over five years and was in charge of her own program in a different location. She was there to observe some of the new developments in that county. We got along well and shared stories, laundry soap, and many of our meals together (she called herself an egg fried rice "expert"). Many of our meals were provided by Elder Brother Wan's wife, who would regularly provide us with a sort of rice gruel: watery rice with some pickled vegetables and the occasional bit of pork. It was tasty and reminded me of breakfasts I had eaten during visits to Taiwan in my childhood.

Next I moved to my own room in the GH "guest quarters," one of a cluster of adjacent buildings that were used as office space, meeting space, and lodging. Some of the rooms in this building were dormitory style (four beds to a room) to accommodate villagers who came for training in agriculture and health care. There was a large shared kitchen where staff boiled water for drinking, prepared meals, and ate together, so I had breakfast and lunch there every day with staff, including an older couple who worked as caretakers of the office complex. Although the director said it was not necessary, I paid 30 RMB ($3.75) per night for lodging in the guest quarters (a hotel in the nearby city was 50 RMB [$6.25] per night). I was regularly invited to dinner gatherings at staff homes. These typically consisted of loosely structured time watching television, eating together, and then watching more television while chatting and snacking. When we dined out together, we took turns paying for the bill, as is the normal practice there for cultivating a friendship.

With the help of the county GH director, and accompanied by people she assigned to help me, I made trips among the township (xiang) offices where I would now spend most of my time. I visited the villages (which roughly surrounded the township buildings) to interview the people there and observe the administration of microfinance programs. In the first township, I roomed with GH staff in a small space with two beds and a chamber pot. In the second, I stayed in a female government official's room in the township complex of buildings by myself; it was roughly twelve by eight feet, had cement floors, and was decorated with a covered clothing rack and stacks of old newspapers. In the third township, I slept on a couch next to a desk in one of the township offices because I didn't feel comfortable in the local bed-and-breakfast (my door didn't lock, and the innkeeper was clearly intoxicated). In the last one, a more prosperous township, I did sleep in the b-and-b (a room designated for guests in the basement of someone's home) for 25 RMB ($3.13) a night. During my time in the townships, I ate my meals with GH staff and the governmental officials who worked with them (as is the custom). We ate either at small restaurants nearby or in the communal dining area if the township had no restaurant. We shared a total of 128 meals. Costs for the meals ranged from 5 to 20 RMB ($0.63 to $2.50). A few times, the dinners included consuming *baijiu*, a potent white wine. I just drank a little, but that was not the norm for the locals – especially the men – who often enjoyed a jolly inebriation. I spent about six months traveling among townships, from which I took sorties (the go-alongs described below) into the villages.

During my last visit to the field site in 2007, I reviewed my findings with the county director at GH (whom I have called Little Wen in this book) a forty-five-minute conversation over a meal. She was interested to hear what I found. As I described my findings, she listened intently, nodding. As we conversed about it, her main question was whether the microfinance programs were destroying social ties in the villages. When I said no, that I thought the borrowers were incorporating microfinance into their existing social ties, she smiled gently. "Oh good," she said, "I just didn't want microfinance to be destroying their social ties (*guanxi*)." I did not have the opportunity to review my findings with villagers or officials, however.

Most of this book draws on data I gathered during go-alongs, interviews, and ethnographic observation. Additionally, I drew on two sources of written documents: microfinance repayment records and GH documents (internal records and reports).

Go-alongs. These systematic, subject-driven outings "follow informants into their familiar environments and track outings they would go on anyway as closely as possible," as recommended by sociologist Margarethe Kusenbach.[1] I went on long hikes, car rides, and ate many meals in community. As sociologist Ashley Mears describes, living with informants and accompanying them on outings gives the researcher a broader sense of how informants understand their situations.[2] I accompanied GH staff and local government officials to trace the social architecture of the poverty-alleviation efforts generally and microfinance specifically. Sometimes I spent full days with staffers in the villages as they distributed money, kept records, and spoke to the villagers about the microfinance programs. Other times, I accompanied staff on shorter (half-day) trips or as they went about everyday tasks in the township offices. My go-alongs lasted anywhere from a few minutes (walking with a staff person down the hall to another room) to seventy-two hours (there were nine outings involving GH staff with whom I spent all day, slept in the same room, ate all meals, and rode on long car rides into the villages). There was very little "down time" to my observations, because even when waiting for rides, taking walks or rides to sites, eating our meals, etc., there was plentiful dialogue.

I had advantages when it came to maneuvering the problem of ethnographic access; the staff generally welcomed my presence. First, the county GH director had already asked them to take me along. Second, the staffers were curious about life in the United States, and I was able to answer questions for them in Chinese. Third, I was both academic and easy-going. They greatly valued education as well as the ability to maintain rapport and a sense of camaraderie. Finally, I was considered low-maintenance; I ate the local food and wasn't picky about lodging. Enjoying the food of the region along with everyone else was particularly important for them as a sign of someone they didn't have to "worry" about. So my own cultural background – especially being ethnically Chinese – provided valuable observational access.

My presence still altered the situation of course. However, when staffers and officials explained to me what they were doing, reflected on how things were going, or vented to me about something that had gone wrong, I was there to catch the interpretations and emotions that informants would not necessarily remember during a sit-down interview later or that might be missed through ethnographic observation alone. Granted, the speaker's focus was necessarily altered by relaying the words to me; they would change what they said in order to better explain what they thought I could understand, or to play to my preferences. But I tried to be as relaxed and low-key as possible. I found that go-alongs with just one individual allowed for the greatest depth of reflections that the person might not share with colleagues around. Meals were an especially good time for people to relax and talk in easy exchange – this is probably true inherently but seemed especially emphasized here.

Go-alongs with more than one person at a time afforded opportunity to observe natural topics of conversation and the tone of discussions. I accompanied groups of GH staff, for example, to the market on weekends to buy fruit and vegetables; then we would go back to the kitchen to cook. During this half-day occupation, lots of conversation topics would naturally come up – about their personal lives and about their work – and it helped me see a fuller picture of their hopes as well as the constraints they felt. Trips to distribute microfinance money in the villages entailed getting into a Jeep with a couple of GH staff, a government official, the driver, and possibly some relatives who appreciated a ride – and spending up to six hours with them on the way. I also observed the staff as a group in the villages during the microfinance meetings.

I jotted down notes in a small notebook and took photos whenever I could, and I had one long field-note-writing session nightly, when I expanded records and mental notes and wrote an account of the day. I had originally intended to use audio recordings but found that the prospect made people nervous. The accuracy lost from foregoing audio recordings was a worthwhile trade-off for gaining people's confidences, as the type of information I was therefore privy to was much more detailed and comprehensive. Because I could access their personal biographies, I could get a sense of how the object of focus (microfinance and third-sector work) fit into their lives. I could see how their work was situated in the space – for example, how GH staffers had to travel to fulfill their jobs and how government officials assigned to the area were "stuck" in rural townships away from friends and family. I could detect and directly observe the way these realities affect perception – the visibility of objects but also how they are interpreted. I was sensitized to what Kusenbach calls the "relevances that govern informants' environmental experiences."[3] I witnessed *in situ* and could compare the filtering and shaping of GH staff and township officials' perceptions, which helped to de-emphasize my own perceptual presuppositions and biases.

Interviews. Over the course of three years, I conducted 118 (individual or group) interviews of 136 people: sixty-three interviews of ninety-three villagers, forty-six interviews of thirty-three microfinance administrators (government officials or GH staff), and nine interviews of ten other people (urban microfinance clients, an owner of a mining company, and an anthropologist). Lasting from thirty minutes to three hours and occurring in offices, homes, and the courtyards of villager homes, the interviews gathered ethnographic data on biographies and daily experiences, especially as related to the microfinance programs.

In addition to the nine go-alongs into the villages, I was in the villages for twenty-one other days, interviewing the residents. The interviews were illuminating, because I could see the social architecture of natural settings in the villages. I saw their homes, how close they were to others, whether people were popping in to watch us talk. I could see, as Kusenbach observed, the "complex web of connections between people, that is, their various relationships, groupings and hierarchies; and they reveal how informants situate themselves in the local social landscape."[4]

My sample of villagers was recruited through GH staff and sometimes township officials; I asked to speak to an equal number of "rich" and "poor" people in the village. I was usually accompanied on my visits: as a friend of GH, I was a legitimate visitor. Some of the time, I interviewed villagers on my own, but often, staffers went with me. GH staff would bring me to the village, where we often met up with their go-between (the village leader). That person would then take us around to visit about four homes a day. Some visits were preplanned, and others were more relaxed; we might simply arrive at a house and see who was home. There was some filtering of people with this, because I didn't know who the village leader was screening out. I would be introduced as a student doing research on development who wants to understand microfinance. I learned to say immediately after the introduction that I was not there to collect repayment, and sometimes the informant visibly relaxed. For the interviews, I used a questionnaire to help guide me, and I took written notes.

Some interviews of GH staffers and government officials happened during my thirty-two-day stay in the GH urban offices, but most of them were during my time at the county or in the townships. These weren't as formally organized as the interviews of the villagers and often occurred during meetings, meals, and lengthy go-alongs. At first, I tried using the questionnaires and taking notes, but I found that the government employees especially felt uncomfortable with this, and regardless, it seemed to be producing more shallow results, even from the GH staffers. I learned to take mental notes instead and to take advantage of access I gained to the government officials I happened to come across – for instance, while obtaining microfinance repayment records, during go-alongs with GH staff, when I was en route to villages, and especially over shared meals.

I replaced all names with pseudonyms and removed potentially identifying information, including geography and dates.

Ethnographic observation. Most of my time was spent doing ethnographic observation at the GH office – I had my own desk in the space, I ate meals with staff, I was included when staff visited each others' homes, and I attended meetings. I also observed microfinance programs being administered in the villages (distribution of money, signing contracts, meetings). My presence meant that things were not completely "natural" in a sense. On the whole, my presence was quite interesting for people at the beginning – particularly that I lived in the United States and was earning a PhD (at the time). Sometimes, villagers who weren't being interviewed also wanted to tell me things and so interrupted an interview to address me or pulled me aside later.

But my opinion is that the initial interest tended to die down – to the benefit of the research – perhaps because I speak Chinese and because in the villages, I did not immediately appear to be a "foreigner." Although a stranger, I didn't look different enough to stir excessive curiosity. They treated me about the same as they would treat a visiting Chinese university student (the distinction between BA and PhD was not important or relevant to them).

Government repayment records. As mentioned, the sixteen administrative villages I examined were located in four townships. The microfinance records for the Grameen-replicator program were kept at the township offices. At three of the offices, with the help of a GH staffer, I was able to obtain permission to examine the written distribution and repayment records. We were not permitted to make copies of the records, but we were allowed to look through the handwritten books. I typed notes about them into a spreadsheet on my laptop computer, using no names. From these notes, the Grameen-replicator repayment rate can be calculated to be around 40 percent (that's 40 percent of the money returned, not 40 percent of the villagers repaying).

The records I viewed did not seem fraudulent, nor did it seem that there were secret records kept somewhere else. However, the records could have caused embarrassment due to the uncovering of lending practices that didn't follow policy. (For instance, how could most villagers repay but only 40 percent of the money get returned? More about this in Chapter 3.)

GH records and reports. Global Hope was forthcoming with their documents and provided me with repayment records (these came from the county level) as well as copies of reports that had been submitted to higher organizational levels. These reports helped me to understand better the goals of the organization and their strategies for poverty alleviation. (Much of the information I received did not apply to microfinance, since microfinance is only a small portion of GH's efforts.)

Glossary

administrative village: formerly "brigade"; the smallest unit of governance in China, an area demarcated by the government ranging in population from one to five thousand that encompasses several natural villages (clusters of households and kinship networks living near each other)

cadre: government personnel – some, members of the Communist Party – who govern rural China at the **township** and **administrative-village** levels and compose the **village committee**, while also working to implement orders from the county level and above (township-level cadres) or living in the village and usually working as a farmer (administrative-village-level cadres)

face (*lian*): respect conferred upon someone with a good reputation as a moral person and a decent human being (which is often understood as one who fulfills obligations)

***guanxi*:** a term frequently used in Chinese language that represents a concept comprising all the connective elements – including both emotional and material components – of personal relationships and social networks

microcredit/microlending: the most well-known type of microfinance (financial services for people with low incomes), which involves the distribution of very small ("micro") loans for the purpose of boosting profit-making among extremely poor people

personhood: the qualities of or conditions for being a human person, defined variously

***renqing* (human feeling):** the understanding of one's own and others' emotional responses to various situations; human obligation[1]

social collateral: as opposed to financial collateral, security derived from social pressure imposed by borrowers on each other to repay a jointly held loan, often employed along with the placing of borrowers into small groups and the making of future loans contingent upon repayment by all group members

township (*xiang*): formerly "commune"; a governing division in China composed of several administrative villages that sits just below the county level and is governed by a mayor, a party secretary (a member of the Chinese Communist Party and often the most powerful decision-making role at any level), and a handful of personnel

village committee (*cunwenhui*): the governing unit of the administrative village whose members collect taxes, play the role of police, document households, implement government policies like family-planning, allocate land, and make decisions about collective enterprises, relief funds, labor contracts, licenses, water and electricity supply, and various other things

Notes

I SOCIAL TIES AND MICROFINANCE

1. Although my main interest in this book is the intersection of social ties, morality, and microfinance, I do not study "religion" in the sense of the comparative religion categories (for example, Buddhist, Christian, Muslim). At present, there is no universally accepted definition of religion for sociologists; whether there is even a distinction between culture and religion is still under debate. This is because it is a surprisingly difficult question. The dictionary definitions of religion (for example, the Cambridge Dictionary, "belief and worship of a god or gods") do not describe major categories of world religions, notably Confucianism (Sun 2013). But the "world religion" categories were themselves constructed in the 1800s in England under the constraints of limited understanding. Though Geertz's (1993, 90) definition of religion as "a system of symbols ... " is widely cited, sociologists of culture have found the conception of "system" to be too rigid to describe both variation between individuals in a society and variation of "beliefs" that an individual can hold at once, at different times, and in response to specific situations (Swidler 2001).

   Hitlin and Vaisey (2013, 55) define "moral" to mean, first, "correspondence with universal standards of right and wrong linked to concerns about justice, fairness, and harm," and second, "understandings of good and bad, right and wrong, worthy and unworthy that vary between persons and between social groups."

   Personhood lies somewhere between the definitions of the religion as a highly structured "system" and of morality as broad understandings of good and bad. Though the conceptions vary dramatically, people have fairly articulated conceptions of what a person is (For a discussion about various concepts of the person, see Chapter 3, pp. 46–49; Chapter 4, pp. 66–69; Chapter 5, pp. 93–95; and Chapter 6, pp. 113–115). Understandings of personhood are consistent symbolic structures that pertain to the metaphysical and cosmological as well as the physical and material.

2. Personhood is a longstanding topic of interest in philosophy (Taylor 1989) that has been given some explicit attention by sociologists recently; see Evans (2016), Smith (2010), and Cahill (1998). I do not argue for any particular view of what a person is, but rather examine the various ways that a person is understood. I treat the person as one of the taken-for-granted features, what Schütz (1953, 1) called "the constructs of common-sense" that are the basis of both scientific thinking and everyday actions. As Schütz (1953, 1) warned, "the so-called concrete facts of common-sense perception are not so concrete as it seems. They already involve abstractions of a highly complicated nature, and we have to take account of this situation lest we commit the fallacy of misplaced concreteness." Therefore I investigate what seems obvious to everyone, what is not necessarily articulated, and the pragmatic base of practical knowledge that people employ without thinking much about it.

Émile Durkheim ([1890]1973, 37) argued that economic and political theory stood on shaky ground because they had been built upon *personne humaine*, a set of doctrines emerging from "the notion of an absolutely autonomous individual, depending only on himself, without historical antecedents, without a social milieu." Durkheim protested that "the individual thus conceived does not exist in reality" and that "the actual man has nothing in common with this abstract entity" (ibid.) Durkheim warned that building theory on an inaccurate concept of the person would lead to faulty models of social life that had nothing to do with how actual people live.

After Durkheim, his nephew Marcel Mauss (1985) also examined the construction of personhood by treating it as a "category of the mind." Since then, two other sets of work have made concepts of the person the basis of their arguments: First, Herbert Simon (1955, 114), in the 1950s and 1960s, argued that it was necessary to get the "model of man" right in order to make more accurate predictions. Rather than the "rational man" of economic theory, people have bounded rationality, and they make decisions in order to "satisfice" – find a course of action that is satisfactory or "good enough." So, Simon argued, "when we substitute for 'economic man' or 'administrative man' a choosing organism of limited knowledge and ability," some of the big questions in theories about organizations disappear. However a person was imagined, this had consequences for economic and organizational theory.

Second, the study of personhood in medicine finds that basic medical theories and categories can be traced back to social-historical set of ideas about what a person is. Lutz calls this "essential difference between emotion and thought" a culturally specific assumption that takes on increased significance when "elevated" and codified with all the power of scientific authority into the categories of "affect" versus "cognition" (Lutz 1988). Then, the division "achieves pathological salience as the difference between affective disorders and thought disorders," two major categories of psychiatric illness whose differences seem to emerge primarily within the cultural settings of Western, and especially American, psychiatry." (Pollock 1996, 321).

The research on cognition is helpful for understanding these mental constructs. The knowledge that is "embedded in human interactions and may not be consciously known," but what "we use to make sense of reality" and "one of the most basic features of automatic cognitive processing," providing "a ready-made way of drawing inferences, although they can also mislead and misjudge" (Patterson 2014, 8). As DiMaggio (1997, 269) writes, schemata "represent objects or events and provide default assumptions about their characteristics, relationships, and entailments under conditions of incomplete information." Schemata are powerful, because people are more likely to perceive information that is germane to existing schemata. They recall schematically embedded information more quickly and more accurately than other input. (Sometimes people even "recall" things according to these schemata that did not actually occur.)

I posit that one type of taken-for-granted knowledge that is embedded in signs and symbols of all participants in microfinance is the concept of the person. If the person is "an identifiable symbolic structure," like other elements of culture (Kaufman 2004, 343), it would be a very powerful one. Since often-used schemata are the basis of new schemata, they are not only present in a set of interactions, but also determine future schemata and interactions. The knowledge activation literature shows that, as Patterson (2014, 19–20) writes, when a knowledge structure is frequently used, "it becomes chronic in the sense that it is the cultural schema that most readily comes to mind in response to social or other environmental stimuli." Schemata are sometimes called "expectancies" by social psychologists, inasmuch as they are mental shortcuts; people organize and process new perceptions in light of these previously stored knowledge structures, which act as tools for survival because they provide useful information rapidly and with little demand on mental processes.

Concepts of personhood vary widely. See Shweder and Bourne (1984) and Markus and Kitayama (1991) for influential works in cultural anthropology and cross-cultural psychology, respectively.

3. Calhoun (1991, 232).
4. Mauss (1985); Shweder and Bourne (1984); Taylor (1989); Gallagher (2011).
5. Calhoun (1991, 233).
6. I draw here from Yan's (1996, 5) discussion of Marcel Mauss.
7. Optimism for microfinance was high from the late 1990s to the mid-2000s, sparking events like the Microcredit Summit in 1997, where delegates from the United Nations and the World Bank, together with individuals such as Bill and Hillary Clinton and megastar Bono, pronounced the goal of alleviating all poverty through the practice of microfinance. In 2006, the Nobel Peace Prize was awarded jointly to Muhammad Yunus and the Grameen Bank for their work in microcredit. By 2010, the total assets in microfinance were estimated at $60 billion, according to Neil MacFarquhar, "Banks Making Big Profits From Tiny Loans," *The New York Times*, April 13, 2010. Accessed November 8, 2015: http://www.nytimes.com/2010/04/14/world/14microfinance.html?pagewanted=all&_r=0. Books like Yunus' (2007) best-selling autobiographical *Banker to the Poor* championed microcredit not only as a source of profit for the poor, but for the lender.

However, microfinance seems to have taken a turn for the worse. In 2008 and 2009, microcredit industries crashed in Bosnia, Morocco, Nicaragua, and Pakistan. Analysts blamed various causes such as debtor revolts and political backlash. In 2010, suicides associated with microcredit repayments in India further tarred the practice. Dispersed case studies also showed the specifics of program failures: A Zambian microfinance institution collapsed while seeking to become a for-profit company (see Juliana Siwale and John Ritchie, 2011, "Failure by Design: The Rise and Fall of a Micro-finance Institution in Zambia – A Case of Pride Zambia." Accessed February 14, 2014: http://eprints.lincoln.ac.uk/5865/2/ 15B.Siwale.format.pdf).

Failures in rural Kyrgyzstan, Bolivia, Peru, Mozambique, and Kenya
were detected (CGAP 2005. "CGAP Case Studies in Agricultural
Microfinance: An Overview." Accessed January 19, 2017: http://docu
ments.worldbank.org/curated/en/528851468198870665/CGAP-case-stu
dies-in-agricultural-microfinance-an-overview).

Randomized studies in India, Mongolia, Morocco, and the Philippines
find that microcredit stimulated activities such as raising chickens or
sewing saris, but the loans did not reduce poverty (Cons and Paprocki
2010). Since incomes are unpredictable, especially for the poor, the money
was often used for survival through unexpected rough patches, rather than
entrepreneurial ventures.

Critiques of microfinance have been made for some time. Morduch's
(2000) work on the microfinance schism foresaw the problem with the
enticing "win-win" proposition that principles of good banking will also
alleviate the most poverty. The rising interest in making microfinance a
profitable business enterprise – as told in books such as business professor
C.K. Pralahad's (2006) *The Fortune at the Bottom of the Pyramid* – reflected
a disheartening turn from poverty alleviation itself, or at least a distracting
interest in making profits for the rich. Roodman's (2012) compelling study
shows that microfinance does exactly what it says it doesn't do: provide
people some extra cash to tide them over when they hit bumps in the road
like a medical crisis, wedding, or funeral. The claim for enabling a family to
"eat for a lifetime" or solving the problem of poverty has not held.

8. Karim (2011).
9. Soutik Biswas. 2010. "India's Micro-Finance Suicide Epidemic." *BBC
   (British Broadcasting Corporation)*. Accessed September 14, 2016: http://
   www.bbc.com/news/world-south-asia-11997571.
10. Collins, Morduch, Rutherford, and Ruthven (2009); Roodman (2012).
    Other studies on microfinance have examined contributions to individual
    empowerment; efficacy in management practices, regulations, and
    policies; and how power structures in microfinance that oppress the
    borrowers. See Campbell (2010); Garikipati, Johnson, Guérin, and Szafarz
    (2017); Barry (2012).
11. Sumner (2010, 21): Table 16 shows the number of people living under
    $1.25 per day in 2007 (in millions): 455.8 in India; 207.5 in China; 88.5 in
    Nigeria; 47.0 in Indonesia; and 11.5 in South Africa. Du (2010, 49) writes
    that, using the definition of living on less than one US dollar per day, there

are currently approximately 130 million people living in poverty in China. If the definition of two US dollars per day is applied, this figure rises to approximately 400 million people.

12. These features describe people living in, for example, Morocco (Rosen 1984), Zimbabwe (Lan 1989), and South Africa (Hickel 2015).

13. "If you want to understand Confucius, read John Dewey. And if you want to understand Dewey, read Confucius," mathematician and philosopher Alfred North Whitehead (2001, 173) wrote. *Guanxi* is consistent with Confucian ideas, which continue to be a big element in Chinese culture. The similarities between *guanxi* and Dewey's theory are likely not coincidental. Dewey, who spent two years in China (1919–21), was very conscious of Chinese philosophy (see Tan 2004, 14–15). Dewey's ([1932] 1985) essay, "The Moral Self," is one example of the consonance between Dewey's writings, Confucian ideas, and everyday Chinese social theory. Dewey wrote that the person "is not something which exists apart from association and intercourse."

14. The *guanxi* view regards everyday life as deeply "configured as a process of social connections," as described by Kleinman and Kleinman (2009, 713).

15. The Chinese *guanxi* can be translated "relationship," "connection," or "personal networks." See King (1991).

16. Ibid., 299.

17. Yang (1994, 68).

18. Yan (2009, 90).

19. I write of the Cartesian and *guanxi*-based perspectives on personhood rather than "Western" and "Chinese" ones for several reasons. Among the 1.3 billion people within the political and geographic borders of the Chinese nation-state, there is variation in the way these people do things. Not only do individuals differ, but also, the same individual is likely to be enacting different concepts of personhood at one time or another; Max Weber (1946, 153) described this when he wrote "Which of the warring gods should we serve?" To say there is one Chinese concept of personhood takes neither type of variation into account. Second, although how people enact personhood in the field site is a subject worthy of attention, this book is merely a study of the how microfinance in rural China intersected with the lives of its borrowers. It cannot do the question justice, because this study does not look at all aspects of the borrowers' lives. Finally, elements of *guanxi*, or something similar to it, have been observed outside

of China, and it is difficult to make claims about what is uniquely Chinese and what is not.

20. Hwang (1987, 949).

21. Dewey ([1932]1985, 296).

22. Kipnis (1997, 16). A son's parents don't have to be still alive for it to matter, because, as Kipnis explains, "reciprocity spans generations and crosses the divide between the living and ancestors."

23. Dewey ([1932]1985, 287).

24. Ibid., 307.

25. Gouldner (1960).

26. Yan (1996).

27. Kleinman and Kleinman (2009, 716); Kleinman (1997, 326).

28. Microfinance researchers have not investigated the social aspects of social collateral, focusing on repayment rates and experimenting with other programmatic aspects instead, such as individual versus group lending; see Gine and Karlan (2014); Kodongo and Kendi (2013). Karim (2011) has a chapter on "the social life of debt," but it is about being in debt more generally, not specifically what the borrowers think of joint liability and what it means in the context of their social, economic, and political environment. Sanyal (2014) is interested in what microfinance meetings do to encourage collective action, not joint liability requirements.

29. I use the term "recipe" to describe a cultural model of cause and effect, after Frye (2012, 1590).

30. I refer to the "third sector" as opposed to "civil society" for empirical precision (Viterna, Clough, and Clarke 2015). I do not use "NGO" or "non-governmental organization" because most global development activities in China require working closely with the local government.

31. Although this book deals with social and cultural norms in relation to microfinance, it does not focus on women's empowerment. Unlike women described in other studies of the topic, the women at this site appeared in public, attended school, worked outside the home, had knowledge of domestic income and control over money, and freely interacted with people outside of family and kin. Microfinance has been appealing to donors because of its claim to women's empowerment and civic participation, which has been supported by some studies, for example Sanyal (2014). On the other hand, a feminist literature criticizes microfinance. Isserles (2003) argues, for example, that the microfinance

rhetoric about women hypocritically *dis*empowers them by affirming a boys-will-be-boys mentality, excusing men's behavior that is detrimental to their families as natural. For issues regarding women's status in rural China, see Bossen (2002).

Although microfinance has also been associated with civic participation and democracy, these aspects are not germane to this field site, given the command of the Chinese Communist Party over the Chinese government. Restrictions on assembly, speech, and demonstration make the kind of civic participation studied elsewhere subject to antisubversion laws here. See, for example, "Rural Unrest in China," *The Economist*, March 15, 2007. Accessed June 20, 2017: http://www.economist.com/node/8864384. As of 2011, 73 percent of the protests made by the rural population were regarding land seizures, according to "Land Seizures Are the Main Cause of Social Unrest in China," *AsiaNews*, December 16, 2010. Accessed March 23, 2011: http://www.asianews.it/news-en/Land-seizures-are-the-main-cause-of-social-unrest-in-China-20273.html.

Finally, although an outsized interest in financial performance has been a major problem in microfinance, leading to the mistreatment of clients and a "loss of moral compass," the problems I describe in this book seemed to occur in tandem with genuinely good intentions. See Hulme and Maitrot (2014).

2   MICROFINANCE IN CHINA

1. Beginning with the 1980s, I use the chronological demarcations laid out in Du (2008a).
2. Liu (2011).
3. Rabinow (1986, 241). I also draw on others who have examined the effect of culture on development. Anthropologist Arturo Escobar asserts that economics inadvertently takes part in a process by which "many other existing conversations or models" are "appropriated, suppressed, or overlooked." Escobar (1995, 62). Many have criticized development economics as a hegemonic tool of oppression. Escobar (1995, 44) writes, "Development was – and continues to be for the most part – a top-down, ethnocentric, and technocratic approach, which treated people and cultures as abstract concepts, statistical figures to be moved up and down in the charts of 'progress.'" I focus on the unintentional aspects of

development, which I suspect play as great a part as the intentional ones in making them "treat people and cultures as abstract concepts."

4. Teets (2014).
5. Li (2011, 2).
6. World Bank (1996).
7. Agricultural Development Bank (2000).
8. CASS is also directed at the top by the government, as all academic institutions are in China. LGOP has executive authority and reported to the State Council, the highest level of government in China.
9. Stiglitz (1990).
10. Besley and Coate (1995, 5).
11. Sun (2010, 15).
12. Park and Ren (2001, 43).
13. Liu (2011, 90).
14. Quoted in Liu (2011, 77).
15. China's Science and Technology Commission 1995 report as cited in Agricultural Development Bank (2000, 7).
16. Jackelen and Xianfeng (1997).
17. Bai (2010, 36).
18. Du (2008b, 23).
19. Du (2008b, 27).
20. Du (2014).
21. Armendáriz and Morduch (2010, 98–9), emphasis mine.
22. Park, Ren, and Wang (2004, 264) find that, among farmers of low wealth in 2000, 10 percent relied on formal loans only, 38 percent relied on informal loans only, and 8 percent relied on both informal and formal loans.
23. Madsen (1984, 93–4).
24. Madsen (1984, 38).
25. Chan, Madsen, and Unger (1992, 26–30). See also Walder (1983).
26. Chung (2014, 594–610).
27. Walder (1983).
28. "Organic Law of the Villagers Committees of the People's Republic of China," National People's Congress. Accessed August 1, 2016: http://www.npc.gov.cn/englishnpc/Law/2007-12/11/content_1383542.htm
29. Yan (2009, 48) gives an example of how cadres can disregard orders from above: "The best example is perhaps their reaction to the campaign of

socialist education launched nationwide in 1990 and 1991 in rural areas ...
but nothing had happened except that some slogans and posters had been
placed on the walls of the village office. Not even a single meeting had
been held for the campaign."

30. Wang (2010, 339).
31. Yan (2009, 32).
32. Adapted from Table 1a in Du (2008a, 6). The original table included the
    eleven types of institutions administering microfinance programs in
    China, the year they began operations, the regions they work in, and their
    target clients, form of collateral, average loan size, annual interest rate,
    number of active clients, gender of clients, value of loans disbursed,
    portfolio quality, and ability to achieve sustainability.
33. Although Du (2008a) lists average loan sizes beginning with several
    thousand RMB, an earlier study article observed programs beginning from
    400 RMB (Park and Ren 2001).
34. As Krause (2014) observes, theories about development and third sector
    organizations sometimes paint relations with the state as inevitably,
    fundamentally confrontational. The third sector is seen as belonging to
    a separate social sphere from the political sphere of the state, with one
    of its main functions to limit government power. This reliance on
    oppositions between good and evil, clean and unclean, has influenced
    the culture of humanitarianism. In the humanitarian field, people see
    things in terms of purity and pollution. The most prominent form of
    perceived pollution is collaboration with the state, which involves
    receiving too much funding from donor governments, implying support
    for a political movement, engaging in politics, or fulfilling part of a
    state's strategic aims. Purity in this context means maintaining a
    distance from government, an impossible task in China given the
    political environment.

3   CREDIT AND FAVOR

1. The daily rate for a day's work, according to my interviews, was 15 RMB
   per day.
2. Chan (2011).
3. Accessed January 6, 2017: http://www.yearofmicrocredit.org/pages/who
   sinvolved/whosinvolved_patronsgroup.asp.

4. Yunus said this with Paul Solman on *The NewsHour with Jim Lehrer* (now *PBS NewsHour*) on November 22, 2006.

5. Collins et al.'s (2009) study of 250 financial diaries kept by people in urban Bangladesh, India, and South Africa found similarly that cash flow is highly variable. People use cash influxes to smooth out income fluctuations and ensure that there is enough money to provide food and other basic requirements on a daily basis. People therefore mix savings and borrowings simultaneously, with sources in informal loans from family and friends, wages, and semiformal or formal loans.

6. Journalist Helen Todd's (1996) inquiry into the lives of sixty-two women in two Bangladeshi villages found that of the forty who had taken microcredit from Grameen Bank, all had stated business plans in order to get their loans: they would buy cows to fatten or rice to husk and resell. A few actually did those things, but most used the money to buy or lease land, repay other loans, stock up on rice for the family, or finance dowries and weddings.

7. Park, Ren, and Wang (2004, 263) report in Table 3 "China Rural Poverty survey Household Credit Use in 1997 and 2000, by Wealth Level (per cent of total new loan value)" that households use credit in this way: 20 percent in production (including fertilizer, livestock, fixed capital, and self-employment), 16 percent consumption (including daily expenditures, weddings and funerals, education, and health), 39 percent for housing, 9 percent to repay other loans, and 14 percent for other.

8. In Rahman's (1999, 120) study, 7 percent of repayment money came from moneylenders, 39 percent from relatives, 2 percent from peers, 9 percent from capital, and 36 percent from profit.

9. Sanyal (2014); Roodman (2012).

10. On the *very small* end of the unit spectrum is a theory of personhood found in early Buddhist texts, where what exists is not a unified soul but rather a cluster of five parts, none of them static: sensations, perceptions, emotions, memories, and volitions. Early Buddhist discourses from the fifth and fourth centuries BCE explain that we use the name "carriage" to describe an object, but in reality, it is a set of wooden parts. Similarly, we use the term "person" to describe ourselves, but we are actually a set of interrelated fragments (Holder 2006). Seeing an individual as a set of "smaller" parts has been an influential perspective for a long time in the social sciences and

humanities. Plato conceptualized personhood as a struggle between one's higher and lower natures. Sigmund Freud, father of psychoanalysis, thought of the individual as consisting of the id, ego, and superego. Philosopher George Herbert Mead (1934) referred to two elements, the "I" and the "me." And sociologist Erving Goffman (1959) points out at least three interacting "selves" in his exposition about "belief in the part one is playing": the self one strives to be, the self one wishes one weren't, and the outcome of the interaction between the two.

11. For example, Malays in Pulau Langkawi conceptualize a person as a set of siblings. The life spirit or essence of a person is the *semangat*, which "is said to be one of seven siblings": "But the seven members of this set do not have any independent existence. They are seven in number, but only one is active. It is as if they formed a kind of sevenfold unity. And this unity is perceived in terms of the sibling relation ... The person is thus both individual and multiple" (Carsten 1995, 227). An example that comes to mind is an orange: It's as if the orange is the sibling group, and the orange sections are individual people. A section all by itself seems somehow disconnected, and it's not what you would picture when someone says "orange." For another example, consider people in the Arunta and Loritja of Australia about a century ago. They pictured a person as two people – a grandson and a grandfather – because they believed that these two shared the same human spirit. Mauss (1985, 11) observed that they use homonyms for grandfather and grandson because they regard a person as being perpetually reborn into the clan. That is, the same word is used to mean grandfather and grandson because they are regarded as literally the same person, reborn.

In sociology, a notable parallel includes Pierre Bourdieu's (1984) notion of the "field" and the perspective of organizational ecology: that specific individuals and social processes are really parts of larger settings. Another is Harrison White's (2008) network perspective on what a person is. For White, identities and positions exist prior to persons, because a person is defined as the intersection at a cluster of social relationships. So the network is the unit of significance, while the person is a node within the network.

12. In the social sciences, a new approach has recently gathered various strands of research together under the umbrella term of "relational

theory." This approach draws on American pragmatists and the empirical work in network analysis. They see the individual identity as actively and constantly being assembled in and through social interactions. The recent discussions understand interpersonal ties as "multiple, fluid, and narratively constructed (and reconstructed) in relation to evolving timeframes" (Mische 2011, 14), and its effort is to investigate the social relationship itself, how people are co-created through their interactions, and fluid (in the process of being created) rather than permanent.

In relational sociology, the primary unit of inquiry is neither the individual nor the system as a whole, but rather the relationships within them. The relationships are so powerful because they are not merely the byproducts of preexisting, discrete, substantive, and material units, but the process by which those individuals come into being. People are not separate from others, but are constituted by their interactions. Individuals do not already know their own interests, then, before they interact. Since relational theories see people as entities whose existence depends on interaction with others, they also see people in a state of flux rather than permanent substances. Relational sociologists have sought to "unfreeze" the static categories that "deny the fluidity" in the patterns of social life (Emirbayer 1997, 308).

13. Among sacred texts, the largest unit for personhood is *all things*. The Bhagavad Gita, composed between the fifth and second century BCE, conveys a theory of personhood common in the Vedanta school of Hindu philosophy through the phrase "Atman is Brahman." This means that there is no distinction between individual souls and the world, or cosmic, soul. The ultimate reality is that the individual is indistinguishable from the all-encompassing unit of *all things*. The Hindu text of the Bhagavad Gita begins with a warrior who is torn because he has been asked to fight with his own relatives. He does not want to do it, but Lord Krishna instructs him on the ultimate true reality, which is that all are one. It is merely an illusion to think that he is fighting his family. The ultimate reality is that *all* is divine, which makes for a very "large" person indeed in that she represents the totality of existence Miller (1986).

14. Rahman (1999).

15. McGregor (1989, 479).

16. Devine (2003, 238).

17. Elyachar (2005).

18. Kipnis (1997, 9).
19. Ferguson (1990, 170).
20. Yan (1996, 63).
21. Simmel ([1900] 1990, 217).
22. Yan (2009, 42).
23. Ibid., 39.
24. For an account of this tension in the 1970s and early 1980s, see Siu (1989). For an account of the late 1990s and early 2000s, see Tsai (2007). For more on birth planning campaigns, see Mueggler (2001) and Mummert (2010).
25. A well-known example is the Beijing mayor and national health minister in the acute respiratory syndrome (SARS) crisis in 2003. See Mei and Pearson (2014, 27).
26. Jackelen, Henry and Mi Xianfeng. 1997. "UNDP Microfinance Assessment Report for China." Accessed September 20, 2016: http://www.sa-dhan.net/Adls/Dl1/Macroeconomics/UNDPMicrofinanceAssessmentReportChina.pdf

4   REPAYING A FRIEND

1. The records for the guarantor program indicated 100 percent repayment, but this must be interpreted in light of the fact that, besides problems with accurate bookkeeping (intentional or unintentional) by program administrators, there was a selection bias: unless a guarantor and his or her assistants were elected and agreed to the terms, the program did not get under way in that area. Therefore the villages where there were social networks that tended to work with the guarantor system were the only ones that were in the sample to begin with.
2. Since Woolcock's (1999) early observations that the nature and extent of social relations (among borrowers, between borrowers and staff, and among staff) can explain failed replications of the same microcredit programs in different places, researchers began paying more attention to the social interactions that accompany microfinance efforts. Researchers have investigated some social variables that affect repayment in microfinance, including group size, caste, and gender. See Manohar and Zeller (1997); Guerin, D'Espallier and Venkatasubramanian (2012); Anthony and Horne (2003); Hung (2003); Ghatak (1999); Morduch (1999). On husband-wife interactions, see Balasubramanian (2013); on group

members talking about personal issues, see Biosca, Lenton, and Mosley (2014); on gender and interactions between loan officers and borrowers, see Rahman (1999). Cardenas and Carpenter (2008) have researched on microfinance that draws from experimental game research between strangers and therefore tries to control for or remove social ties entirely: if friends or relatives show up for an experiment together, they are assigned to different sessions in an attempt to uncover universal principles about the game.

3. Portes and Sensenbrenner (1993); Small (2009); Parry and Bloch (1989).

4. Adam Smith's explanation of sympathy in *Theory of Moral Sentiments* features a self that is so enclosed that apart from the conscious activity of imagination, the viewing even of torture should have little effect on the individual. While Smith does have hope of human identification with misery, in order for sympathy to make sense to him, he delineates a rather slow process that requires a mental exercise to bridge a gap – the gap between self and other – that is understood to be vast:

> As we have no immediate experience of what other men feel, we can form no idea of the manner in which they are affected, but by conceiving what we ourselves should feel in the like situation. Though our brother is upon the rack, as long as we ourselves are at our ease, our senses will never inform us of what he suffers. They never did, and never can, carry us beyond our own person, and it is by the imagination only that we can form any conception of what are his sensations ... By the imagination we place ourselves in this situation, we conceive ourselves enduring all the same torments, we enter as it were into his body, and become in some measure the same person with him, and thence form some idea of his sensations, and even feel something which, though weaker in degree, is not altogether unlike them. His agonies, when they are thus brought home to ourselves, when we have thus adopted and made them our own, begin at last to affect us, and we then tremble and shudder at the thought of what he feels.
>
> *(1976, 9)*

Smith's ideas contrast with those of Mencius (372–289 BCE), one of the most important interpreters of Confucianism, who developed the idea that a basic and innate part of human nature is to be able to understand and share in the feelings of others. In his example of the stranger seeing a small child on the verge of falling into a well, Mencius describes an immediate reaction – a sudden sense of fright and dismay – that transcends conscious reasoning. This feeling, Mencius argues, does not arise, really, from the desire to silence the unpleasant screams of the child, win praise from friends, or ingratiate oneself with the child's parents. On the contrary, someone who did not instantly rush to save the child would "simply not be a person." Unlike Mencius' famous example of the child at the precipice of a well, in Smith's explanation we can only be affected after we pretend like something is happening to us. This pretending happens slowly and with deliberation, like a conversion. The site of action is deeply internal: "In every passion of which the mind of man is susceptible, the emotions of the by-stander always correspond to what, *by bringing the case home to himself,* he imagines should be the sentiments of the sufferer" (Smith 1976, 9; my emphasis).

In contrast, there is a body of research philosophy, religion, and psychology that studies the boundary between self and other in terms of "oneness." See Ivanhoe et al. (2017). An individual, to Smith, is surrounded by a thick curtain which only very unreliable and infrequent sensory "imaginations" penetrate. And even these must be brought in. Only once in the internal place (the site of action) do they affect the individual. Otherwise, you can see out of the curtain, but you can only wonder what the things outside of the curtain are like.

Smith's view on separation is extreme. There are people on the other extreme who feel that there are no curtains at all separating them from others – one person is thought of to be literally the same person as another.

Tamil pilgrims in the 1980s had the goal of experiencing the "other" in such immediacy that it would no longer seem clear where the self ends and others begin. This is knowledge of the truth, the merging with the universal soul, or *brahman.* This is the point at which the pilgrim says, "Now I really know" (Daniel 1984, 286).

5. Cooley (1992, 152).
6. Dewey ([1932]1985, 299).
7. Ibid.
8. Ibid., 300.
9. Ibid., 301.
10. Gold, Guthrie, and Wank (2002, 10).
11. Tu (1981, 45–7).
12. Carpenter, Daniere, and Takahashi (2004).

13. Goffman (1959).
14. Zhu (2000, 207).
15. As Coleman (1988) wrote, this kind of cross-cutting relationship, which he called "multiplex relations," has the effect of increasing scrutiny and – in his observations, preventing high school students at Catholic schools from dropping out.
16. Orsi (1985, 85): The self that thus took shape in the domus, nurtured and formed most fundamentally by its values, was also revealed there. This is where people declared who they were, where they identified themselves as human beings. The *domus* in Italian Harlem was a theater of self-revelation: on this stage, a person showed the world his or her worth and integrity, responsibility, and devotion, the respect they gave and the respect they were due.
17. Goffman (1959).
18. Coleman (1988, S105).
19. Hsu (2014).
20. Yang (1994, 69).
21. Oxfeld (2010, 4).
22. In the field site, like other places in rural China, the local officials kept careful track of all the comings and goings of people in the area. Visitors from the outside were either legitimate or illegitimate. Legitimate visitors included visiting officials, or, in my case, being a friend of GH. Illegitimate ones would most certainly be questioned and followed. As a friend of GH, I was treated with little or no scrutiny. At times, I roamed on my own, but at others, a staffer accompanied me. My impression was that the staffers seemed more preoccupied with being a good host than with surveillance.
23. Shun (1993).
24. Other colorful names that stuck in the village included "Dog Penis" (*gou laojing*) – because he was wild as a boy, stole public vegetables and grains, and was involved in gangs. Later, his family took on this name, too. Zhu (2000, 206).

5   THE SOCIAL COST OF SANCTIONS

1. Madsen (1984, 212) describes how people synthesized Confucian tradition with Maoist ideas in the 1950s to form an ethos of courage, heroism, generosity, good human "feeling," and "serving the people." But through

the 1960s, Mao pushed through rapid collectivization and the Great Leap Forward. Then, in the face of economic failure, he attempted to reassert his power by appealing to moral heroism to extremes in the Cultural Revolution, when people were urged to struggle passionately against class enemies while they did not have enough food to eat. People became disillusioned with such moral ideals and politics. In the 1970s and 1980s, a kind of pragmatism emerged, emphasizing balance and dutiful obedience to the bureaucratic regulations issued by higher-level authorities. This site in the early 2000s seemed to show the same, at least for the ordinary villager.

2. Yan (1996).

3. The interest in permanence – the unchanging aspects of a person – was strong in Plato's treatment of the soul and in Aristotle's focus on the principles of human nature. And although Augustine reserved a sense of change in his understanding of the soul, his work paved the way for Descartes' imagination of the person, composed primarily of the mind and free will, who did not experience change (Taylor 1989, 118). The social sciences took up a "model of man," to use Simon's (1955) term again, that is essentially fixed. A contrast is the Confucian emphasis on how a person undergoes slow change through the decades, as this passage from *The Analects* describes:

At fifteen, I committed myself to learning.
At thirty, I stood firm.
At forty, I had no doubts.
At fifty, I understood the decree of Heaven.
At sixty, my ear was attuned.
At seventy, I followed my heart's desires without overstepping propriety (Analects 2.4).

American pragmatism offered a consonant view.

The ability to comprehend the changing person agrees with people in many other times and places. Among the Southern Tswana in South Africa in the 1970s, an elderly woman was described as "not yet" having children, even though she was past childbearing age, because people saw a person as a continuous, cumulative series of actions. To say "she never had children" would be to place the woman's life in the past tense; regardless of her age, the woman was still in the process of becoming.

Comaroff and Comaroff (2001, 271) report that "among Southern Tswana, the creation of a conjugal bond, and of the parties to it as fully social adults, took the form of a protracted, cumulative succession of exchanges, sometimes ending only after the death of the spouses. What is more, the status of that bond was always open to (re)interpretation – as casual sex, concubinage (*bonyatsi*), living together (*ba dula mmogo*), marriage (*nyalo*) – this being facilitated by the fact that the terms used between partners (*monna* [m], *mosadi* [f]) were unmarked; they might as well have referred to someone with whom an individual cohabited the night before as to a mate of long-standing. Nor, in the flow of everyday life, was any effort made to clarify such things: relations might go undefined because, in the normal course of events, they were growing, developing, becoming. As were the human beings involved in them. It was only at moments of rupture, when the continuing present came to an abrupt end, that there was any necessity to decide what they *had been*. Or, rather, had become."

4. Menary (2011, 621), writing of James.
5. Dewey ([1932]1985, 307).
6. Ibid., 304.
7. Ibid., 306.
8. Zhu (2000, 296).
9. Astuti (1995); Carsten (1995).
10. Karim (2011, xvi).
11. Ibid., xviii.
12. Michelson (2007, 460).
13. Cho (2003).
14. Yan (2009, 47).
15. Zhu (2000, 203).
16. Ibid., 204.
17. Ibid., 216.
18. Goffman (1959, 102–3).

6   PRAGMATISM AND THE SOCIOLOGY OF DEVELOPMENT

1. Soutik Biswas, 2010. "India's Micro-Finance Suicide Epidemic." *BBC (British Broadcasting Corporation)*. Accessed September 14, 2016: http://www.bbc.com/news/world-south-asia-11997571.

2. Escobar (1995, 59): "The economy is not only, or even principally, a material entity. It is above all a cultural production, a way of producing human subjects and social orders of a certain kind."

3. Go (2017, 196).

4. Granovetter (1985); Zelizer (2012); Bandelj (2012).

5. Viterna (2013).

6. Tavory and Swidler (2009).

7. Originating in the United Nations Development Programme, the HDI is intended to measure changes in human well-being by tracking three factors: GDP per capita, expected years of schooling for an individual and mean years of schooling for a society, and life expectancy at birth for an individual. Since 2010, two changes to the index have weighted the social dimension a little more heavily: including the mean years of schooling in a society, and calculating an Inequality-adjusted Human Development Index (IHDI).

8. Nussbaum (2011, 33–4). I paraphrase her list here:

   1. A normal lifespan and one worth living.
   2. Bodily health, including food and shelter.
   3. Freedom to make choices about one's own body – where you go, what you do, how and when you have sex.
   4. The ability to imagine and think.
   5. The ability to experience emotion and connection to others.
   6. The ability to reason and plan.
   7. The ability to affiliate and interact freely with others.
   8. An awareness of one's relationship to other species.
   9. The ability to play and enjoy life.
   10. Reasonable control over one's property and environment.

9. Gasper (2007, 336).

10. Hickel (2015, 215) argues that Nussbaum's list echoes Western legal thought.

11. Richardson (2006).

12. Weber (1978).

13. Peter Evans' (1995) work has given rise to an enormous amount of research from this perspective.

14. Mahoney (2010); Whyte (2009).

15. Marx (1972).

16. Wallerstein (1974); Chase-Dunn (1989).

17. Wuthnow (1987, 23).

18. Menary (2011).

19. Durkheim ([1898]1973, 37–40 and 47–9).

20. Vaillant (2012) describes the Grant Study, or the Harvard Study of Adult Development, which began in 1938 with the goal of learning about optimum health and potential, and the conditions that promote it. For the study, 268 male students were chosen from the Harvard College classes of 1939, 1940, and 1941, and followed for seventy-five years (and counting). Who would "make it to ninety years of age, physically capable and mentally alert; who would build lasting and happy marriages; who would achieve conventional (or unconventional) career success"? (2). The study shows a correlation between the warmth of one's parental relationships to health and happiness in old age. In particular, it is the warmth of relationship to their mothers that led to earning more and lower likelihood of developing dementia. Warm childhood relationships with fathers correlated with lower anxiety and increased life satisfaction at age seventy-five. Vaillant writes, "The seventy-five years and twenty million dollars expended on the Grant Study points ... to a straightforward five-word conclusion: 'Happiness is love. Full stop'" (2012, 52).

21. Escobar (1995, 155) writes of how development expanded to include farmers in the 1960s, women in the 1970s, and nature in the 1980s. This panoptic gaze is an apparatus of social control by mapping people into particular spaces.

22. Swidler and Watkins (2009).

23. Dewey ([1932]1985, 291).

24. Ferguson (2013).

25. Hickel (2015).

26. This ability to shape oneself is the basis of Dewey's definition of freedom: "In the degree in which we become aware of possibilities of development and actively concerned to keep the avenues of growth open, in the degree in which we fight against induration and fixity, and thereby realize the possibilities of recreation of our selves, we are actually free." See Dewey ([1932]1985, 306).

27. Frye (2012, 1567); Tavory (2016, 62).

28. Wolford (2006).

APPENDIX: FIELDWORK METHODOLOGY

1. Kusenbach (2003, 463).
2. Mears (2015, 1104).
3. Kusenbach (2003, 469).
4. Ibid., 466.

GLOSSARY

1. Yan (1996, 122) defines *renqing* this way: " ... the term *renqing* connotes a
wide range of meanings and can hardly be translated into a single English
word. In common usage *renqing* embraces four different yet related
meanings. First, it means human feelings – the basic emotional responses of
an individual in confrontation with various daily life situations. In this first
meaning, *renqing* is social in nature and requires that one have an
understanding of others' emotional responses in accordance with his or her
own. Second, *renqing* indicates a set of social norms and moral obligations.
These norms and obligations require keeping in contact with those of one's
guanxi network and participating in the exchange of gifts, greetings, visits,
and assistance. Third, in its extended usage *renqing* can be regarded as a
kind of resource, such as a favor or a gift, and can be used as a medium of
social exchange. Finally, in certain contexts, *renqing* is used as a synonym
for *guanxi*. People may talk about how much *renqing* they possess when in
fact they are referring to the size of their *guanxi* networks."

Bibliography

Agricultural Development Bank. 2000. "A Study on Ways to Support Poverty Reduction Projects (ADB/TA 3150-PRC)." Available at: www.people.fas.harvard.edu/~ces/people/pdf/Support_Poverty_Reduction_Projects_China.pdf.

Anthony, Denise, and Christine Horne. 2003. "Gender and Cooperation: Explaining Loan Repayment in Micro-Credit Groups." *Social Psychology Quarterly* 66: 293–302.

Armendáriz, Beatriz, and Jonathan Morduch. 2010. *The Economics of Microfinance*. Cambridge: MIT Press.

Astuti, Rita. 1995. *People of the Sea: Identity and Descent among the Vezo of Madagascar*. New York: Cambridge University Press.

Bai, Chengyu. 2010. "Chinese Microfinance Networks and Cooperation Patterns." *Microfinance in China*. World Microfinance Forum Geneva: 32–41. Available at: www.microfinancegateway.org/sites/default/files/mfg-en-paper-microfinance-in-china-mar-2010.pdf.

Balasubramanian, Sujata. 2013. "Why Micro-Credit May Leave Women Worse Off: Non-Cooperative Bargaining and the Marriage Game in South Asia." *Journal of Development Studies* 49: 609–23.

Bandelj, Nina. 2012. "Relational Work and Economic Sociology." *Politics & Society* 40 (2): 175–201.

Barry, Jack J. 2012. "Microfinance, the Market and Political Development in the Internet Age." *Third World Quarterly* 33(1): 125–41.

Bellah, Robert, Richard Madsen, William Sullivan, Ann Swidler, and Steven Tipton. 1985. *Habits of the Heart: Individualism and Commitent in American Life*. Berkeley: University of California Press.

Besley, Timothy, and Stephen Coate. 1995. "Group Lending, Repayment Incentives and Social Collateral." *Journal of Development Economics* 46 (1): 1–18.

Biosca, Olga, Pamela Lenton, and Paul Mosley. 2014. "Where Is the 'Plus' in 'Credit-Plus'? The Case of Chiapas, Mexico." *Journal of Development Studies* 50: 1700–16.

Bossen, Laurel. 2002. *Chinese Women and Rural Development: Sixty Years of Change in Lu Village, Yunnan*. New York: Rowman & Littlefield.

Bottomore, T.B. 1964. *Karl Marx: Selected Writings in Sociology and Social Philosophy*. New York: McGraw-Hill.

Bourdieu, Pierre. 1984. *Distinction: A Social Critique of the Judgment of Taste*. London: Routledge.

Bourdieu, Pierre. 1990. *The Logic of Practice*. Trans. Richard Nice. Stanford: Stanford University Press.

Cahill, Spencer. 1998. "Toward a Sociology of the Person." *Sociological Theory* 16(2): 131–48.

Calhoun, Craig. 1991. "Morality, Identity, and Historical Explanation: Charles Taylor on the Sources of the Self." *Sociological Theory* 9(2): 232–63.

Campbell, Gregor. 2010. "Microfinancing the Developing World: How Small Loans Empower Local Economies and Catalyse Neoliberalism's Endgame." *Third World Quarterly* 31(7):1081–90.

Cardenas, Juan Camilo, and Jeffrey Carpenter. 2008. "Behavioural Development Economics: Lessons from Field Labs in the Developing World." *Journal of Development Studies* 44: 311–38.

Carpenter, Jeffrey, Amrita Daniere, and Lois Takahashi. 2004. "Cooperation, Trust, and Social Capital in Southeast Asian Urban Slums." *Journal of Economic Behavior & Organization* 55: 533–51.

Carsten, Janet. 1995. "The Substance of Kinship and the Heat of the Hearth: Feeding, Personhood, and Relatedness among Malays in Pulau Langkawi." *American Ethnologist* 22(2): 223–41.

Chan, Anita, Richard Madsen, and Jonathan Unger. 1992. *Chen Village Under Mao and Deng*. Berkeley: University of California Press.

Chan, Kam Wing. 2013. "China: Internal Migration." In *The Encyclopedia of Global Human Migration*, eds. Immanuel Ness and Peter Bellwood. Oxford: Blackwell Publishing. Available at: http://onlinelibrary.wiley.com/doi/10.1002/9781444351071.wbeghm124/full.

Chase-Dunn, Christopher. 1989. *Global Formation: Structures of the World-Economy*. Oxford: Basil Blackwell.

Cho, Young Nam. 2003. "Symbiotic Neighbour or Extra-Court Judge? The Supervision over Courts by Chinese Local People's Congresses." *The China Quarterly* 176: 1068–83.

Chung, Him. 2014. "Rural Transformation and the Persistence of Rurality in China." *Eurasian Geography and Economics* 54: 594–610.

Coleman, James. 1988. "Social Capital in the Creation of Human Capital." *American Journal of Sociology* 94: S95–S121.

Collins, Daryl, Jonathan Morduch, Stuart Rutherford, and Orlanda Ruthven. 2009. *Portfolios of the Poor: How the World's Poor Live on $2 a Day.* Princeton: Princeton University Press.

Comaroff, John, and Jean Comaroff. 2001. "On Personhood: An Anthropological Perspective from Africa." *Social Identities* 7: 167–283.

Confucius. 1979. *The Analects.* New York: Penguin.

Cons, Jason, and Paprocki, Kasia. 2010. "Contested Credit Landscapes: Microcredit, Self-Help and Self-Determination in Rural Bangladesh." *Third World Quarterly* 31 (4): 637–54.

Cooley, Charles Horton. 1992. *Human Nature and the Social Order.* New York: Transaction Publishers.

Daniel, E. Valentine. 1984. *Fluid Signs: Being a Person the Tamil Way.* Berkeley: University of California Press.

Devine, Joseph. 2003. "The Paradox of Sustainability: Reflections on NGOs in Bangladesh." *Annals of the American Academy of Political and Social Science* 590: 227–42.

Dewey, John. [1932]1985. "15. The Moral Self." *The Collected Works of John Dewey, 1882–1953.* Electronic Edition: 285–311. The Later Works of John Dewey, 1925–1953. Volume 7: 1932, Ethics.

DiMaggio, Paul. 1997. "Culture and Cognition." *Annual Review of Sociology* 23: 263–87.

Du, Xiaoshan. 2008a. "The Current Situation and Future Prospects for Microfinance in China." *Microfinance in China.* World Microfinance Forum Geneva: 2–9. Available at: www.microfinancegateway.org/library/current-situation-and-future-prospects-microfinance-china.

Du, Xiaoshan. 2008b. "The Current Supply of Microfinance Savings in China," *Microfinance in China.* World Microfinance Forum Geneva: 22–31. Available at: www.microfinancegateway.org/library/current-situation-and-future-prospects-microfinance-china.

Du, Xiaoshan. 2014. "Reflections on microfinance and risk management from Mr. Du Xiaoshan, Chairman of China Microfinance Association." Available at: www.microfinancegateway.org/sites/default/files/mfg-en-paper-reflections-on-microfinance-and-risk-management-interview-with-the-chairman-of-china-microfinance-association-mar-2014.pdf.

Durkheim, Émile. [1890]1973. "Individualism and the Intellectuals." *On Morality and Society.* Trans. Mark Traugott. Edited and with an introduction by Robert Bellah. Chicago: University of Chicago Press: 43–57. Originally published as "L'individualisme et les intellectuels," Revue bleue 4e: 7–13.

Durkheim, Émile. [1898]1973. "The Principles of 1789 and Sociology." *On Morality and Society*. Trans. Mark Traugott. Edited and with an introduction by Robert Bellah. Chicago: University of Chicago Press: 34–42. Originally published as "Les principes de 1789 et la sociologie," *Revue international de l'enseignement* 19: 450–66.

Elyachar, Julia. 2005. *Markets of Dispossession: NGOs, Economic Development and the State in Cairo*. Durham, NC: Duke University Press.

Emirbayer, Mustafa. 1997. "Manifesto for a Relational Sociology." *American Journal of Sociology* 103 (2): 281–317.

Escobar, Arturo. 1995. *Encountering Development: The Making and Unmaking of the Third World*. Princeton: Princeton University Press.

Evans, John. 2016. *What Is a Human? What the Answers Mean for Human Rights*. New York: Oxford University Press.

Evans, Peter. 1995. *Embedded Autonomy: States and Industrial Transformation*. Princeton: Princeton University Press.

Ferguson, James. 1990. *The Anti-Politics Machine: "Development," Depoliticization, and Bureaucratic Power in Lesotho*. New Haven: Yale University Press.

Ferguson, James. 2013. "Declarations of Dependence: Labour, Personhood, and Welfare in Southern Africa." *Journal of the Royal Anthropological Institute* 19: 226–7.

Frye, Margaret. 2012. "Bright Futures in Malawi's New Dawn: Educational Aspirations as Assertions of Identity." *American Journal of Sociology* 117(6): 1565–1624.

Gallagher, Shaun. 2011. "Introduction: A Diversity of Selves." *Oxford Handbook of the Self*, ed. Shaun Gallagher. New York: Oxford University Press: 1–29.

Garikipati, Supriya, Susan Johnson, Isabelle Guérin, and Ariane Szafarz. 2017. "Microfinance and Gender: Issues, Challenges and the Road Ahead." *The Journal of Development Studies* 53(5): 641.

Gasper, Des. 2007. "What Is the Capability Approach? Its Core, Rationale, Partners and Dangers." *The Journal of Socio-Economics* 36: 335–59.

Geertz, Clifford. [1987] 1993. "Religion as a Cultural System." *The Interpretation of Cultures: Selected Essays*. New York: Basic Books: 87–125.

Ghatak, Maitreesh. 1999. "Group Lending, Local Information and Peer Selection." *Journal of Development Economics* 60: 27–50.

Giné, Xavier and Dean Karlan. 2014. "Group versus Individual Liability: Short and Long Evidence from Philippine Microcredit Lending Groups." *Journal of Development Economics* 107: 65–83.

Go, Julian. 2017. "Decolonizing Sociology: Epistemic Inequality and Sociological Thought." *Social Problems* 64: 194–99.

Goffman, Erving. 1959. *The Presentation of Self in Everyday Life.* New York: Doubleday.

Gold, Thomas, Doug Guthrie, and David Wank. 2002. "An Introduction to the Study of *Guanxi.*" *Social Connections in China: Institutions, Culture, and the Changing Nature of Guanxi,* eds. Thomas Gold, Doug Guthrie, and David Wank. New York: Cambridge University Press: 3–20.

Gouldner, Alvin. 1960. "The Norm of Reciprocity: A Preliminary Statement." *American Sociological Review* 25: 161–78.

Granovetter, Mark. 1985. "Economic Action and Social Structure: The Problem of Embeddedness." *American Journal of Sociology* 91: 481–510.

Guerin, Isabelle, Bert D'Espallier, and Govindan Venkatasubramanian. 2012. "Debt in Rural South India: Fragmentation, Social Regulation and Discrimination." *Journal of Development Studies* 49: 1155–71.

Hickel, Jason. 2015. *Democracy as Death: The Moral Order of Anti-Liberal Politics in South Africa.* Berkeley: University of California Press.

Hitlin, Steven, and Stephen Vaisey. 2013. "The New Sociology of Morality." *Annual Review of Sociology* 39: 51–68.

Holder, John J., ed. and trans. 2006. "The Greater Discourse on the Foundations of Mindfulness," Digha Nikaya 2.290–315. *Early Buddhist Discourses.* Indianapolis: Hackett Publishing Company: 42–58.

Hsu, Becky. 2014. "Alleviating Poverty or Reinforcing Inequality? Interpreting Micro-Finance in Practice, with Illustrations from Rural China." *The British Journal of Sociology* 65: 245–65.

Hulme, David, and Mathilde Maitrot. 2014. "Has Microfinance Lost Its Moral Compass?" *Economic & Political Weekly XLIX* (48): 77–85.

Hung, Chikan Richard. 2003. "Loan Performance of Group-Based Microcredit Programs in the United States." *Economic Development Quarterly* 17: 382–95.

Hwang, Kwang-kuo. 1987. "Face and Favor: The Chinese Power Game." *American Journal of Sociology* 92(4): 944–74.

Isserles, Robin. 2003. "Microcredit: The Rhetoric of Empowerment, the Reality of 'Development as Usual.'" *Women's Studies Quarterly* 31 (3/4): 38–57.

Ivanhoe, Philip J., Owen Flanagan, Victoria Harrison, Eric Schwitzgebel, and Hagop Sarkissian (eds). 2017. *Oneness in Philosophy, Religion, and Psychology.* New York: Columbia University Press.

Jackelen, Henry and Mi Xianfeng. 1997. "UNDP Microfinance Assessment Report for China." Accessed September 20, 2016: Available at: www.sa-dhan.net/Adls/Dll/Macroeconomics/UNDPMicrofinanceAssessmentReportChina.pdf.

Joas, Hans. 2001. *The Genesis of Values*. Trans. Gregory Moore. Chicago: University of Chicago Press.

Karim, Lamia. 2011. *Microfinance and Its Discontents*. Minneapolis: University of Minnesota Press.

Kaufman, Jason. 2004. "Endogenous Explanation in the Sociology of Culture." *Annual Review of Sociology* 30: 335–57.

King, Ambrose. 1991. "Kuan-hsi [guanxi] and Network Building: A Sociological Interpretation." *Daedalus* 120 (2): 63–84.

Kipnis, Andrew. 1997. *Producing* Guanxi: *Sentiment, Self, and Subculture in a North China Village*. Durham: Duke University Press.

Kleinman, Arthur, and Joan Kleinman. 2009. "How Bodies Remember: Social Memory and Bodily Experience of Criticism, Resistance, and Delegitimation following China's Cultural Revolution." *New Literary History* 25(3): 707–23.

Kleinman, Arthur. 1997. "'Everything That Really Matters': Social Suffering, Subjectivity, and the Remaking of Human Experience in a Disordering World." *Harvard Theological Review* 3: 315–35.

Kusenbach, Margarethe. 2003. "Street Phenomenology: The Go-Along as Ethnographic Research Tool." *Ethnography* 4(3): 455–85.

Lan, David. 1989. "Resistance to the Present by the Past: Mediums and Money in Zimbabwe." *Money and the Morality of Exchange*, eds. Jonathan Parry and Maurice Bloch. Cambridge: Cambridge University Press: 191–208.

Li, Yuwen. 2011. "Introduction: Challenges and Opportunities for NGOs in Different Parts of the World." *NGOs in China and Europe: Comparisons and Contrasts*, ed. Yuwen Li. Surrey: Ashgate: 1–22.

Liu, Peifeng. 2011. "Development of Charities in China Since the Reform and Opening Up." *NGOs in China and Europe: Comparisons and Contrasts*, ed. Yuwen Li. Surrey: Ashgate: 71–94.

Lizardo, Omar, and Jessica Collett. 2013. "Embarrassment and Social Organization: A Multiple Identities Model." *Social Forces* 92 (1): 353–75.

Lutz, Catherine. 1988. *Unnatural Emotions*. Chicago: University of Chicago Press.

Madsen, Richard. 1984. *Morality and Power in a Chinese Village*. Berkeley: University of California Press.

Mahoney, James. 2010. *Colonialism and Postcolonial Development: Spanish America in Comparative Perspective*. New York: Cambridge University Press.

Markus, Hazel Rose and Shinobu Kitayama. 1991. "Culture and the Self: Implications for Cognition, Emotion, and Motivation." *Psychological Review* 98 (2): 224–53.

Marx, Karl. 1972. *The Marx-Engels reader*. Vol. 4. New York: Norton.

Mauss, Marcel. 1967. *The Gift: Forms and Functions of Exchange in Archaic Societies,* trans. E.E. Evans-Pritchard. New York: Norton.

Mauss, Marcel. 1985. "A Category of the Human Mind: The Notion of Person; The Notion of Self." *The Category of the Person: Anthropology, Philosophy, History,* eds. Michael Carrithers, Steven Collins, and Steven Lukes. Cambridge: Cambridge University Press: 1–25.

McGregor, J. Allister. 1989. "Towards a Better Understanding of Credit in Rural Development." *Journal of International Development* 1 (4): 467–86.

Mead, George Herbert. 1934. *Mind, Self, and Society.* Ed. Charles W. Morris. Chicago: University of Chicago Press.

Mears, Ashley. 2015. "Working for Free in the VIP: Relational Work and the Production of Consent." *American Sociological Review* 80(6): 1099–1122.

Mei, Ciqi and Margaret Pearson. 2014. "Diffusion of Policy Defiance among Chinese Local Officials." *Local Governance Innovation in China: Experimentation, diffusion, and defiance,* eds. Jessica Teets and William Hurst. London: Routledge: 25–41.

Menary, Richard. 2011. "Our Glassy Essence: The Fallible Self in Pragmatist Thought." *Oxford Handbook of the Self,* ed. Shaun Gallagher. New York: Oxford: 609–32.

Meyer, John W., and Brian Rowan. 1977. "Institutionalized Organizations: Formal Structure as Myth and Ceremony." *The American Journal of Sociology* 83(2): 340–63.

Meyer, John. 2010. "World Society, Institutional Theories, and the Actor." *Annual Review of Sociology* 36: 1–20.

Michelson, Ethan. 2007. "Climbing the Dispute Pagoda: Grievances and Appeals to the Official Justice System in Rural China." *American Sociological Review* 72: 459–85.

Miller, Barbara Stoler, trans. 1986. *The Bhagavad Gita: Krishna's Counsel in Time of War.* New York: Bantam Dell.

Mische Ann. 2011. "Relational Sociology, Culture, and Agency." *Sage Handbook of Social Network Analysis,* eds. John Scott and Peter Carrington. New York: Sage: 80–97.

Morduch, Jonathan. 1999. "The Microfinance Promise." *Journal of Economic Literature* 37: 1569–614.

Morduch, Jonathan. 2000. "The Microfinance Schism." *World Development* 28: 617–29.

Mosse, David. 2005. *Cultivating Development: An Ethnography of Aid Policy and Practice.* London: Pluto Press.

Mueggler, Erik. 2001. *The Age of Wild Ghosts: Memory, Violence, and Place in Southwest China*. Berkeley: University of California Press.

Mummert, Gail. 2010. "Growing Up and Growing Old in Rural Mexico and China: Care-giving for the Young and the Elderly at the Family-State Interface." *Rural Transformations and Development-China in Context: The Everyday Lives of Policies and People*, eds. Norman Long, Jingzhong Ye, and Yihuan Wang. Northhampton: Edward Elgar Publishing: 215–52.

Nussbaum, Martha. 2011. *Creating Capabilities: The Human Development Approach*. Cambridge: Harvard University Press.

Orsi, Robert. 1985. *The Madonna of 115th Street: Faith and Community in Italian Harlem, 1880–1950*. New Haven: Yale University Press.

Oxfeld, Ellen. 2010. *Drink Water, But Remember the Source: Moral Discourse in a Chinese Village*. Berkeley: University of California Press.

Park, Albert, and Changqing Ren. 2001. "Microfinance with Chinese Characteristics." *World Development* 29: 39–62.

Park, Albert, Changqing Ren, and Sangui Wang. 2004. "Micro-finance, Poverty Alleviation, and Financial Reform in China." *Rural Finance and Credit Infrastructure in China*, eds. Stefan Tangermann and William Witherell. Paris: Organisation for Economic Co-Operation and Development (OECD): 256–83.

Parry, Jonathan and Maurice Bloch. 1989. "Introduction: Money and the Morality of Exchange." *Money and the Morality of Exchange*, eds. Jonathan Parry and Maurice Bloch. Cambridge: Cambridge University Press: 1–32.

Patterson, Orlando. 2014. "Making Sense of Culture." *Annual Review of Sociology* 40: 1–30.

Pollock, Donald. 1996. "Personhood and Illness among the Kulina." *Medical Anthropology Quarterly* 10(3): 319–41.

Portes, Alejandro, and Julia Sensenbrenner. 1993. "Embeddedness and Immigration: Notes on the Social Determinants of Economic Action." *American Journal of Sociology* 98 (6): 1320–50.

Rabinow, Paul. 1986. "Representations Are Social Facts: Modernity and Post-Modernity in Anthropology." *Writing Culture: The Poetics and Politics of Ethnography*, eds. James Clifford and George Marcus. Berkeley: University of California Press: 234–61.

Radelet, Steven. 2015. "The Rise of the World's Poorest Countries." *Journal of Democracy* 26 (4): 5–19.

Rahman, Aminur. 1999. *Women and Microcredit in Rural Bangladesh: Anthropological Study of the Rhetoric and Realities of Grameen Bank Lending*. Boulder: Westview Press.

Richardson, Henry. 2006. "Rawlsian Social-Contract Theory and the Severely Disabled." *The Journal of Ethics* 10 (4): 419–62.

Roodman, David. 2012. *Due Diligence: An Impertinent Inquiry into Microfinance.* Washington, DC: Center for Global Development Books.

Rosen, Lawrence. 1984. *Bargaining for Reality: The Construction of Social Relations in a Muslim Community.* Chicago: University of Chicago Press.

Sanyal, Paromita. 2014. *Credit to Capabilities: A Sociological Study of Microcredit Groups in India.* New York: Cambridge University Press.

Schütz, Alfred. 1953. "Common-Sense and Scientific Interpretation of Human Action." *Philosophy and Phenomenological Research* 14(1): 1–38.

Sen, Amartya. 1977. "Rational Fools: A Critique of the Behavioral Foundations of Economic Theory." *Philosophy and Public Affairs* 6(4): 317–44.

Sen, Amartya. 1999. *Development as Freedom.* New York: Oxford University Press.

Sharma, Manohar, and Manfred Zeller. 1997. "Repayment Performance in Group-Based Credit Programs in Bangladesh: An Empirical Analysis." *World Development* 25: 1731–42.

Shun, Kwong-loi. 1993. "Jen and Li in the 'Analects.'" *Philosophy East and West* 43 (3): 457–79.

Shweder, Richard, and Edmund Bourne. 1984. "Does the Concept of the Person Vary Cross Culturally?" *Culture Theory: Essays on Mind, Self and Emotion*, eds. R. Shweder and R. LeVine. Cambridge: Cambridge University Press: 158–99.

Simmel, Georg. [1900] 1990. *The Philosophy of Money.* Ed. David Frisby; Trans. Tom Bottomore and David Frisby. New York: Routledge.

Simon, Herbert A. 1955. "A Behavioral Model of Rational Choice." *The Quarterly Journal of Economics* 69(1): 99–118.

Siu, Helen. 1989. *Agents and Victims in South China: Accomplices in Rural Revolution.* New Haven: Yale University Press.

Small, Mario. 2009. *Unanticipated Gains: Origins of Network Inequality in Everyday Life.* New York: Oxford University Press.

Smith, Adam. 1976. *The Theory of Moral Sentiments.* Eds. D.D. Raphael and A.L. Macfie Oxford: Clarendon Press.

Smith, Christian. 2010. *What Is a Person?: Rethinking Humanity, Social Life, and the Moral Good from the Person Up.* Chicago: University of Chicago Press.

Stiglitz, Joseph. 1990. "Peer Monitoring and Credit Markets." *World Bank Economic Review* 4: 351–66.

Sumner, Andy. 2010. *Global Poverty and the New Bottom Billion: Three–Quarters of the World's Poor Live in Middle–Income Countries.* Brighton: Institute of Development Studies.

Sun, Anna. 2013. *Confucianism as a World Religion: Contested Histories and Contemporary Realities*. Princeton: Princeton University Press.

Sun, Tongquan. 2010. "The Policy and Legal Framework for Microfinance in China," *Microfinance in China*, 10–15. Accessed August 3, 2016: Available at: www.microfinancegateway.org/sites/default/files/mfg-en-paper-microfinance-in-china-mar-2010.pdf.

Swidler, Ann, and Susan Cotts Watkins. 2009. "'Teach a Man to Fish': The Doctrine of Sustainability and Its Effects on Three Strata of Malawian Society." *World Development* 37 (7): 1182–96.

Swidler, Ann. 2001. *Talk of Love: How Culture Matters*. Chicago: University of Chicago Press.

Swidler, Ann. 2009. "Dialectics of Patronage: Logics of Accountability at the African AIDS-NGO Interface." *Globalization, Philanthropy, and Civil Society: Projecting Institutional Logics Abroad*, eds. David Hammack and Steven Heydemann. Bloomington: Indiana University Press: 192–220.

Tan, Sor-hoon. 2004. *Confucian Democracy: A Deweyan Reconstruction*. Albany: State University of New York Press.

Tavory, Iddo. 2016. *Summoning: Identification and Religious Life in a Jewish Neighborhood*. Chicago: University of Chicago Press.

Tavory, Iddo, and Ann Swidler. 2009. "Condom Semiotics: Meaning and Condom Use in Rural Malawi." *American Sociological Review* 74(2): 171–189.

Taylor, Charles. 1989. *Sources of the Self: The Making of the Modern Identity*. Cambridge: Harvard University Press.

Teets, Jessica. 2014. *Civil Society under Authoritarianism: The China Model*. New York: Cambridge University Press.

Todd, Helen. 1996. *Women At the Center: Grameen Bank Borrowers after One Decade*. Boulder: Westview Press.

Tsai, Lily. 2007. *Accountability without Democracy: Solidary Groups and Public Goods Provision in Rural China*. New York: Cambridge University Press.

Tu, Wei-Ming. 1981. "Jen [ren] as a Living Metaphor in the Confucian Analects." *Philosophy East and West* 31 (1): 45–54.

Vaillant, George. 2012. *Triumphs of Experience*. Cambridge: Harvard University Press.

Viterna, Jocelyn, Emily Clough, and Killian Clarke. 2015. "Reclaiming the "Third Sector" from "Civil Society." *Sociology of Development* 1 (1): 173–207.

Viterna, Jocelyn. 2013. *Women in War: The Micro-Processes of Mobilization in El Salvador*. New York: Oxford University Press.

Walder, Andrew. 1983. "Organized Dependency and Cultures of Authority in Chinese Industry." *Journal of Asian Studies* XLIII(1): 51–76.

Wallerstein, Immanuel. 1974. *The Modern World System I: Capitalist Agriculture and the Origins of the European World-Economy in the Sixteenth Century.* New York: Academic.

Wang, Fei-Ling. 2010. "Renovating the Great Floodgate: The Reform of China's Hukou System." *One Country, Two Societies: Rural-Urban Inequality in Contemporary China,* ed. Martin King Whyte. Cambridge: Harvard University Press: 335–66

Weber, Max. 1946. *From Max Weber: Essays in Sociology.* New York: Oxford University Press.

Weber, Max. 1978. *Economy and Society: An Outline of Interpretive Sociology.* Berkeley: University of California Press.

White, Harrison C. 2008. *Identity and Control: A Structural Theory of Social Action.* Princeton: Princeton University Press.

Whitehead, Alfred North. 2001. *Dialogues of Alfred North Whitehead.* Ed. Lucien Price. Boston: David R. Godine Publisher.

Whyte, Martin King. 2009. "Paradoxes of China's economic boom," *Annual Review of Sociology* 35: 371–92.

Wiley, Norbert. 2006. "Pragmatism and the Dialogical Self." *International Journal of Dialogical Science* 1 (1): 5–21.

Wolford, Wendy. 2006. "The Difference Ethnography Can Make: Understanding Social Mobilization and Development in the Brazilian Northeast." *Qualitative Sociology* 29 (3): 335–52.

Woolcock, Michael. 1999. "Learning from Failures in Microfinance: What Unsuccessful Cases Tell Us about How Group-Based Programs Work." *The American Journal of Economics and Sociology* 58: 17–42.

World Bank. 1996. "Microfinance and Poverty Alleviation: United Nations Collaboration with Chinese Experiments". Accessed September 19, 2016. Available at: www.microfinancegateway.org/sites/default/files/mfg-en-paper-m icrofinance-and-poverty-alleviation-united-nations-collaboration-with-chinese -experiments-1996.pdf.

Wuthnow, Robert. 1987. *Meaning and Moral Order: Explorations in Cultural Analysis.* Berkeley: University of California Press.

Wuthnow, Robert. 2009. *Boundless Faith: The Global Outreach of American Churches.* Berkeley: University of California Press.

Yan, Yunxiang. 1996. *The Flow of Gifts: Reciprocity and Social Networks in a Chinese Village.* Stanford: Stanford University Press.

Yan, Yunxiang. 2009. *The Individualization of Chinese Society.* London: Berg Publishers.

Yanagisako, Silvia, and Jane Collier. 1989. *Gender and Kinship: Toward a Unified Analysis*. Stanford: Stanford University Press.

Yang, Mayfair. 1994. *Gifts, Favors, and Banquets: The Art of Social Relationships in China*. Ithaca: Cornell University Press.

Zelizer, Viviana. 2012. "How I Became a Relational Economic Sociologist and What Does That Mean?" *Politics & Society* 40(2): 145–74.

Zhu, Xiaoyang. 2000. "Punishment in a Chinese Village in Yunnan." PhD diss., Macquarie University.

Index

STUDIES OF THE WEATHERHEAD EAST ASIAN INSTITUTE

Columbia University

Selected Titles
(Complete list at: www.columbia.edu/cu/weai/weatherhead-studies.html)

Mobilizing Without the Masses: Control and Contention in China, by Diana Fu. Cambridge University Press, 2017.

Inheritance of Loss: China, Japan, and the Political Economy of Redemption After Empire, by Yukiko Koga. University of Chicago Press, 2016.

Negotiating Rural Land Ownership in Southwest China: State, Village, Family, by Yi Wu. University of Hawaii Press, 2016.

The Age of Irreverence: A New History of Laughter in China, by Christopher Rea. University of California Press, 2015.

The Nature of Knowledge and the Knowledge of Nature in Early Modern Japan, by Federico Marcon. University of Chicago Press, 2015.

The Fascist Effect: Japan and Italy, 1915–1952, by Reto Hoffman. Cornell University Press, 2015.

The International Minimum: Creativity and Contradiction in Japan's Global Engagement, 1933–1964, by Jessamyn R. Abel. University of Hawai'i Press, 2015.

Empires of Coal: Fueling China's Entry into the Modern World Order, 1860–1920, by Shellen Xiao Wu. Stanford University Press, 2015.

Casualties of History: Wounded Japanese Servicemen and the Second World War, by Lee K. Pennington. Cornell University Press, 2015.

City of Virtues: Nanjing in an Age of Utopian Visions, by Chuck Wooldridge. University of Washington Press, 2015.

The Proletarian Wave: Literature and Leftist Culture in Colonial Korea, 1910–1945, by Sunyoung Park. Harvard University Asia Center, 2015.

Neither Donkey Nor Horse: Medicine in the Struggle Over China's Modernity, by Sean Hsiang-lin Lei. University of Chicago Press, 2014.

When the Future Disappears: The Modernist Imagination in Late Colonial Korea, by Janet Poole. Columbia University Press, 2014.

Bad Water: Nature, Pollution, & Politics in Japan, 1870–1950, by Robert Stolz. Duke University Press, 2014.

Rise of a Japanese Chinatown: Yokohama, 1894–1972, by Eric C. Han. Harvard University Asia Center, 2014.

Beyond the Metropolis: Second Cities and Modern Life in Interwar Japan, by Louise Young. University of California Press, 2013.

From Cultures of War to Cultures of Peace: War and Peace Museums in Japan, China, and South Korea, by Takashi Yoshida. MerwinAsia, 2013.

Imperial Eclipse: Japan's Strategic Thinking about Continental Asia before August 1945, by Yukiko Koshiro. Cornell University Press, 2013.

The Nature of the Beasts: Empire and Exhibition at the Tokyo Imperial Zoo, by Ian J. Miller. University of California Press, 2013.

Public Properties: Museums in Imperial Japan, by Noriko Aso. Duke University Press, 2013.

Reconstructing Bodies: Biomedicine, Health, and Nation-Building in South Korea Since 1945, by John P. DiMoia. Stanford University Press, 2013.

Taming Tibet: Landscape Transformation and the Gift of Chinese Development, by Emily T. Yeh. Cornell University Press, 2013.

Tyranny of the Weak: North Korea and the World, 1950–1992, by Charles K. Armstrong. Cornell University Press, 2013.

The Art of Censorship in Postwar Japan, by Kirsten Cather. University of Hawai'i Press, 2012.

Asia for the Asians: China in the Lives of Five Meiji Japanese, by Paula Harrell. MerwinAsia, 2012.

Lin Shu, Inc.: Translation and the Making of Modern Chinese Culture, by Michael Gibbs Hill. Oxford University Press, 2012.

Occupying Power: Sex Workers and Servicemen in Postwar Japan, by Sarah Kovner. Stanford University Press, 2012.

Redacted: The Archives of Censorship in Postwar Japan, by Jonathan E. Abel. University of California Press, 2012.

Empire of Dogs: Canines, Japan, and the Making of the Modern Imperial World, by Aaron Herald Skabelund. Cornell University Press, 2011.

Planning for Empire: Reform Bureaucrats and the Japanese Wartime State, by Janis Mimura. Cornell University Press, 2011.

Behind the Gate: Inventing Students in Beijing, by Fabio Lanza. Columbia University Press, 2010.